Dane Love is the author of numerous books on Scotland in general and on Ayrshire in particular. He was born in Cumnock but now lives in the countryside near Auchinleck. He is descended from Robin Love, who fought for Bonnie Prince Charlie at the battles of Prestonpans and Culloden. A member of Ayrshire Archaeological and Natural History Society, he is also the Honorary Secretary of the Scottish Covenanter Memorials Association and a Fellow of the Society of Antiquaries of Scotland. He works as a Principal Teacher at Irvine Royal Academy. In his free time, he enjoys travelling around Scotland with his wife and two children, visiting historic sites and doing research.

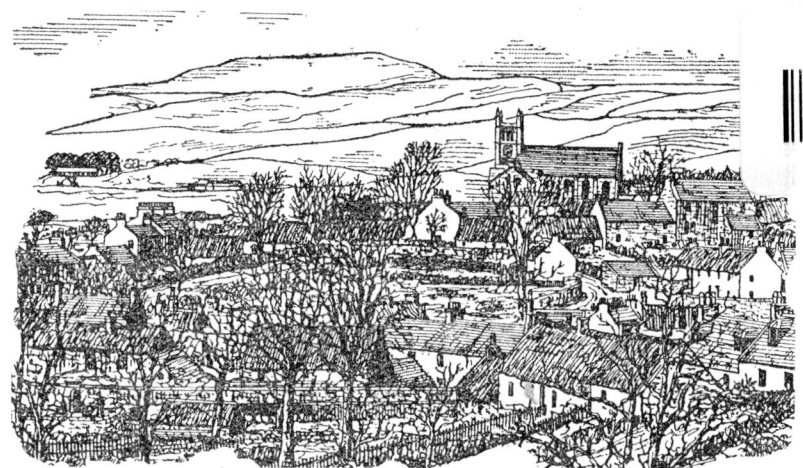

Sketch of Dalmellington in 1902

Title Page and Back Cover: Ordnance Survey Six Inch Map of Dalmellington of 1860.
Following Page: A view of Waterside Street and Cathcartston, looking to the Muck Bridge.

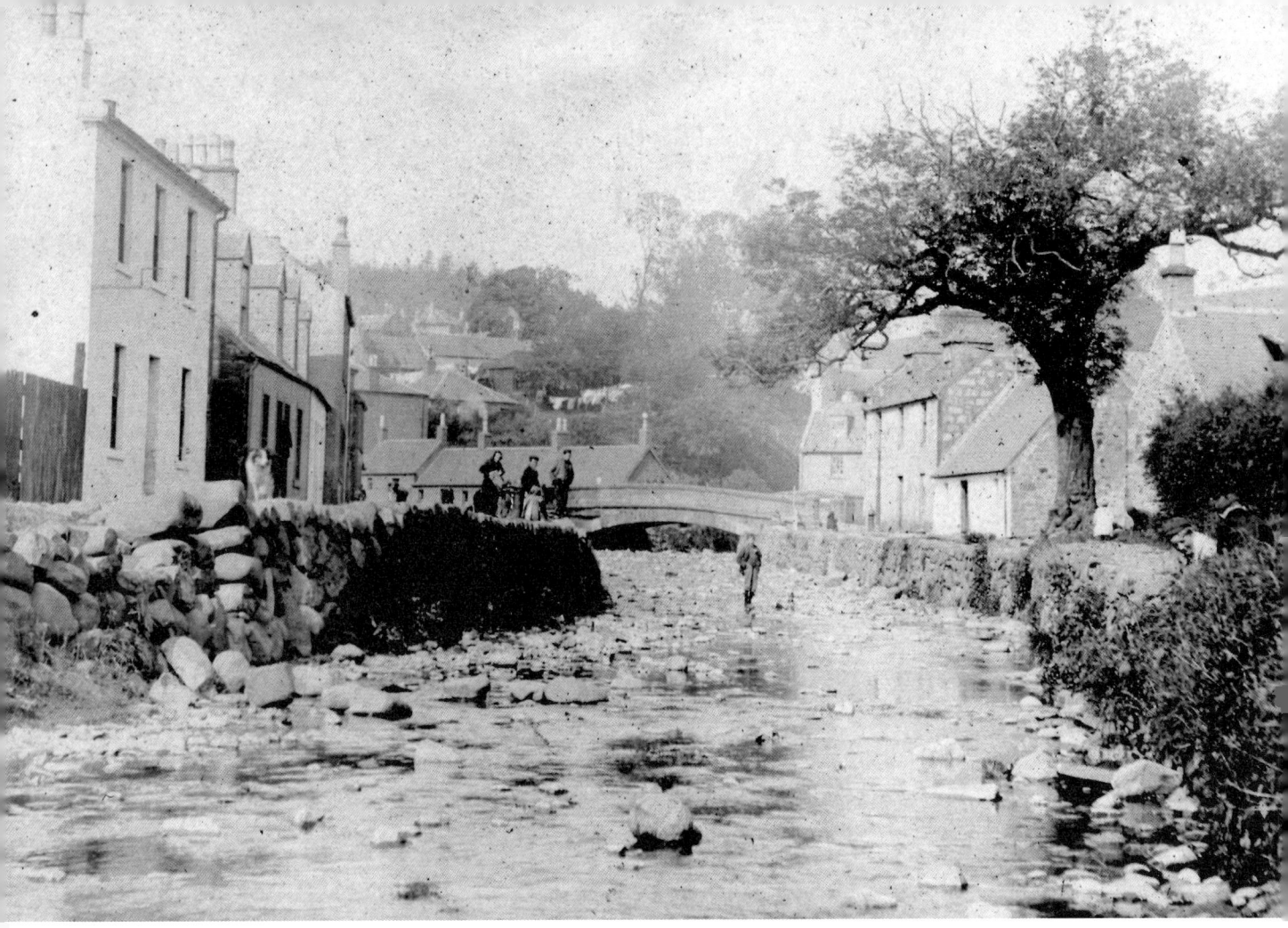

A Look Back at DALMELLINGTON

Dane Love

CARN PUBLISHING

© Dane Love, 2017.
First Published in Great Britain, 2017.

ISBN - 978 1 9110430 3 4

Published by Carn Publishing,
Lochnoran House,
Auchinleck,
Ayrshire, KA18 3JW.

www.carnpublishing.com

Printed by Bell & Bain Ltd.,
Glasgow, G46 7UQ.

The right of the author to be identified as the author of this work has been asserted by him in accordance with the Copyright, Designs and Patents Act, 1988.

All rights reserved. No part of this publication can be reproduced, stored, or transmitted in any form, or by any means, electronic, mechanical or photocopying, recording or otherwise, without the express written permission of the publisher.

Introduction

The village of Dalmellington was established near to the ancient motte hill, a place of defence which would have controlled much of the surrounding countryside. The motte is sixty feet diameter on its top and on the side facing Castlecroft it has a protective ditch. The motte survives, but its surmounting tower has long gone. The community survived, becoming a small market centre for the district. In 1373 Sir Duncan Wallace of Sundrum received a charter to the Barony of Dalmellington, which was passed to his nephew, Sir Alan de Cathcart, ancestor of the Craigengillan family. In 1501 the church was annexed by James IV to the Chapel Royal at Stirling, and the chapel there supplied preachers. On 4 March 1607, the village was created a Free Burgh of Barony by James VI, officially titled the Castlemerk of Dalmellington. The village originated on the south side of the Muck Burn, known as Dalmellington Town. The village expanded across the burn, forming Dalmellington Mains, perhaps in the early eighteenth century. Certainly, General Roy's map of 1747-55 shows little building across the water.

Dalmellington played an active part in the Covenanting struggle of 1638-1689. Many locals supported the Covenant, and notable Covenanters were Roger Dun (1659-1689) of Benquhat, John Paterson (1650-1740) of Pennyvenie, Quintin Dick and Hugh Hutchison. To try to quell suspected rebellion and to root out Covenanting sympathisers, a garrison of soldiers was established in the village. Similarly, in 1678, nine hundred highlanders were billeted here. In 1679 two Dalmellington men, Hugh Simpson and Walter Humper, were drowned when the ship taking them to the Americas as slaves was wrecked in the Orkney islands. Three other locals escaped from the wreck.

In the eighteenth century, the village was a centre for weaving, with a number of weavers plying their trade in the typical cottages of their time – thatched, single-storey, and having a room for the loom. Weavers' agents travelled back and forth from the village with orders, taking away the finished cloth. In the town were a few small woollen mills, the sheep-covered hills around the village being a ready source of wool. One of these stood off the Path, built by Wright, Colville & Co. in the 1790s. The other was behind the Dalmellington Inn, which existed from before 1795, being valued at £300 at that time. This mill was later owned by William Cameron, a minor song-writer, noted for 'Jessie o' the Dale' and 'Dinna Cross the Burn, Willie.'

Woollen mills were established in the late eighteenth century and operated until the early twentieth century. Around 1900 there were two small woollen mills in operation, employing around thirty people. The yarn that was spun was sent to Kilmarnock for use in the carpet factories. One of the mill owners opened a carpet factory with eight looms, the other made blankets, plaids and packing cloth.

One of the old mill buildings was converted into a small hospital, in existence in the 1850s. This was closed around 1900 and a new hospital was opened near the junction of Gateside Road with Burnton Road, roughly where an old ironstone pit had existed.

Around 1800 there were plans to build a canal through Dalmellington, linking the village with Kirkcudbright, but these never materialised. The village was connected with the outside world with the arrival of the railway in 1856, but again plans to continue this to Galloway never materialised.

A public water supply was established in the village by Mrs MacAdam Cathcart, who instructed James MacDerment, civil engineer, of Ayr, to form a reservoir at the top of the Gas Brae and lay pipes to pumps. A dozen wells were erected, the work completed by James Wyllie, contractor.

Much of Dalmellington and the surrounding countryside was for decades part of Craigengillan estate, the mansion house being located across the River Doon, in Straiton parish. The MacAdam Cathcart family, who owned it, played an important part in the history and development of the village, and their burial vault is located in the centre of the old churchyard. In 1919 much of the estate was sold, breaking it up considerably, with Bellsbank lands being acquired by the tenant, John Walker, and Pennyvenie by the Dalmellington Iron Company. The motte hill was sold to R. Welsh, solicitor, for £70.

It was in 1847 that the community started to change its outlook and become prosperous in a way that it had never experienced before. Although coal was worked on a small scale for many years, the lack of a large market meant that it was only burned on local fires. The Dalmellington Ironworks were established a few miles down the glen at Waterside, but the resulting demand for ironstone, coal and limestone meant that there were insufficient workers in the parish to excavate the raw materials from the ground. Thousands of men and their families descended on the area from all over Britain and Ireland, and soon miners' rows and other houses had to be built to accommodate them.

Mines were sunk all around the parish, and in the immediate locality of the village, these existed at Pennyvenie (the oldest pit sunk in 1868), Sillyhole (from 1845),

Minnivey (1848), Chalmerson (1860s), and Craigmark (from 1866). Ironstone pits also existed, some as close to the village centre as the one next to Sillyhole Bridge, on Gateside Road, in operation in the 1850s. At Dalmellington, a coal preparation plant was created with an overhead cableway bringing coal from Bogton pit. With a massive influx of workers from Ireland and elsewhere in Scotland, the village expanded, and with it the number of businesses which were established to supply the needs of the population.

The village grew with the removal of a number of surrounding mining villages, such as Craigmark and Benquhat. The houses at Broomknowe were erected in 1910, Burnton in 1924 and Bellsbank Crescent in 1929. Other places where the village expanded included Castlecrofts, Dalton Avenue and Park Crescent. A new community was established at Bellsbank from 1948.

Deep-mining stopped in the late 1900s, but the working of coal continued for a number of decades by open-cast means. However, the considerable number of workers employed locally has plummeted, resulting in a falling population. The population of Dalmellington has risen and fallen over the years. In 1845, just as the industrial revolution was taking place in the valley, the village had around 800 residents. In 1881 the village had 1,437 residents, rising to 2,900 in 1951. In 2001 its population was 1,407 plus a further 1,619 living at Bellsbank.

A community spirit thrives in the village. The Craigengillan Curling Club was founded on 3 December 1841, Masonic Lodge St Thomas in 1864, Dalmellington Band in 1864, Dalmellington Bowling Club in 1875, the 33rd Ayrshire Scouts in 1910, and Craigmark Burntonians Football Club in 1929.

Today, Dalmellington is a village that is trying to re-invent itself. Old buildings that are surplus to requirement have been removed, though it is unfortunate that a number of historical structures have been lost in the process. In 1998 the village was designated as a 'book town', the former school being leased in 2000, but it didn't manage to keep up with Wigtown in this respect and it no longer claims this title. The open-cast coal mines that scarred the hillsides north of the village have closed, the demand for coal having fallen, and industry is difficult to attract. What the future for the village will be is difficult to ascertain.

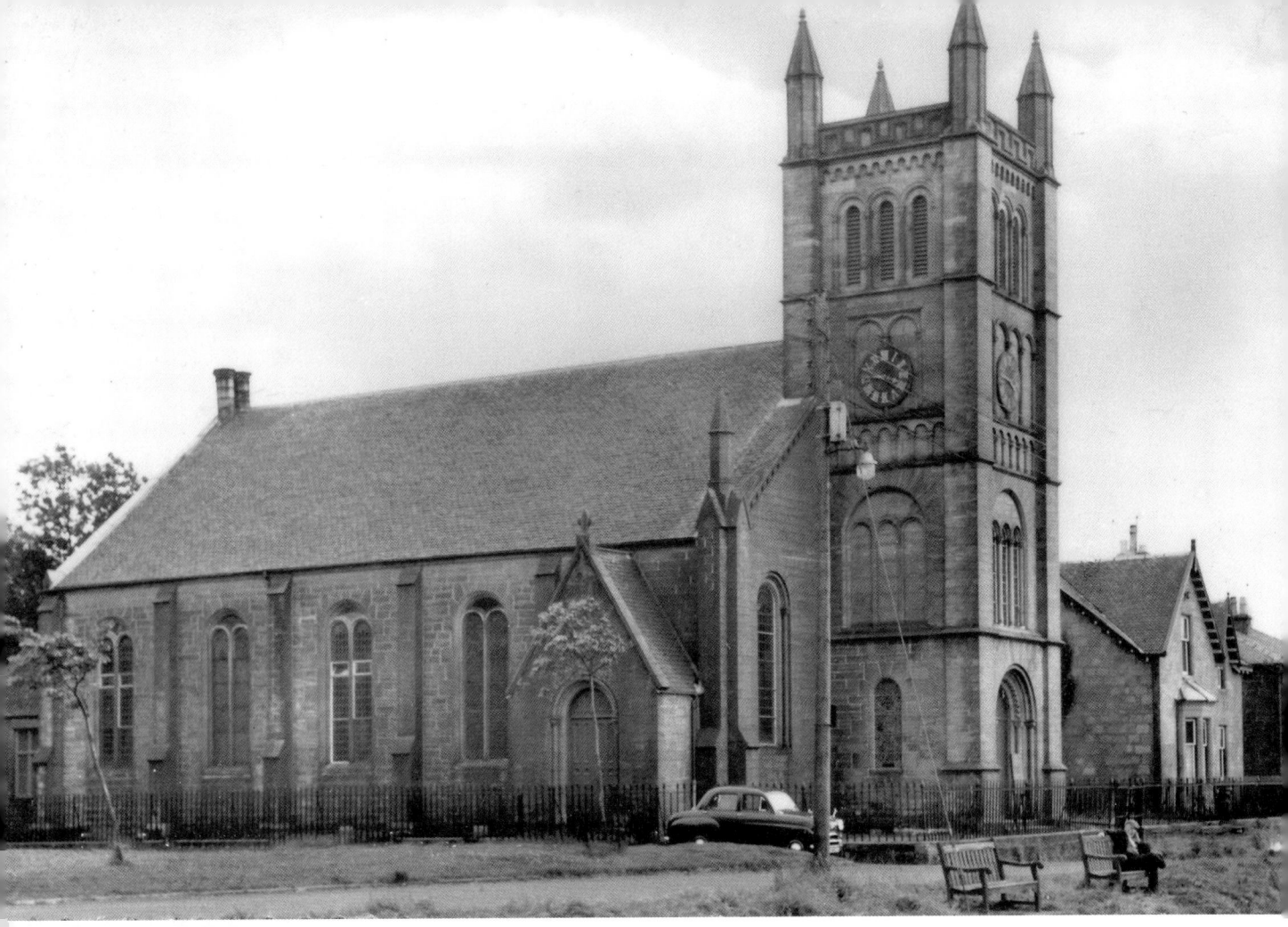

Kirk o' the Covenant

Perched on an elevated hill above the village, Dalmellington Parish Church is seen from miles around as one approaches Dalmellington. The church was erected in 1845-6 to replace the old parish church, which was located further along the Windy Raw. The architect of the building was Patrick Wilson of Edinburgh, who produced a typical neo-Norman design, the tower adding to the prominence of the site. The stone for the building was quarried at Dunaskin. The church was gifted by Mrs MacAdam Cathcart and Hon. Colonel F. MacAdam Cathcart of Craigengillan and was opened on 18 October 1846. The Cathcarts had the sole use of the gallery and the tower room. Originally, the church had 640 sittings.

In 1869 there were proposals to light the church by gas, and in 1872 matting for the nave floor was gifted. In 1875 the church changed its style of worship, replacing standing for prayer and singing whilst seated with standing to sing and kneeling for prayers. In 1881 an 'instrument' was presented to the church to accompany the singing, and the session noted that 'no objections have been taken to its introduction.' In 1901 the congregation was so big that plans were drawn up to extend the church by adding new transepts, side galleries and opening up the tower room. These plans did not materialise.

The church was renovated internally in 1937, when the pews from Old Greyfriars in Edinburgh were installed. There are many fine stained glass windows, the work of A. Ballantine and Gardiner, Gordon Webster and Marjorie Kemp. Memorials commemorate former members of the congregation, including Captain John Woodburn (1802-1841) and Sir John Woodburn (1843-1902). Captain John was killed in Afghanistan and is commemorated in St John's Church, Bombay. Sir John was the Lieutenant Governor of Bengal and died in Calcutta, where a statue commemorates him.

The church was known as the Kirk o' the Covenant, when the union of the United Free and Church of Scotland resulted in two parish churches in Dalmellington, then three when Bellsbank Parish Church was opened. In 1983 Lamloch Parish Church united with the parish church. Locals claim that the door of the church is painted red to commemorate the blood shed by the Covenanter martyrs of the parish.

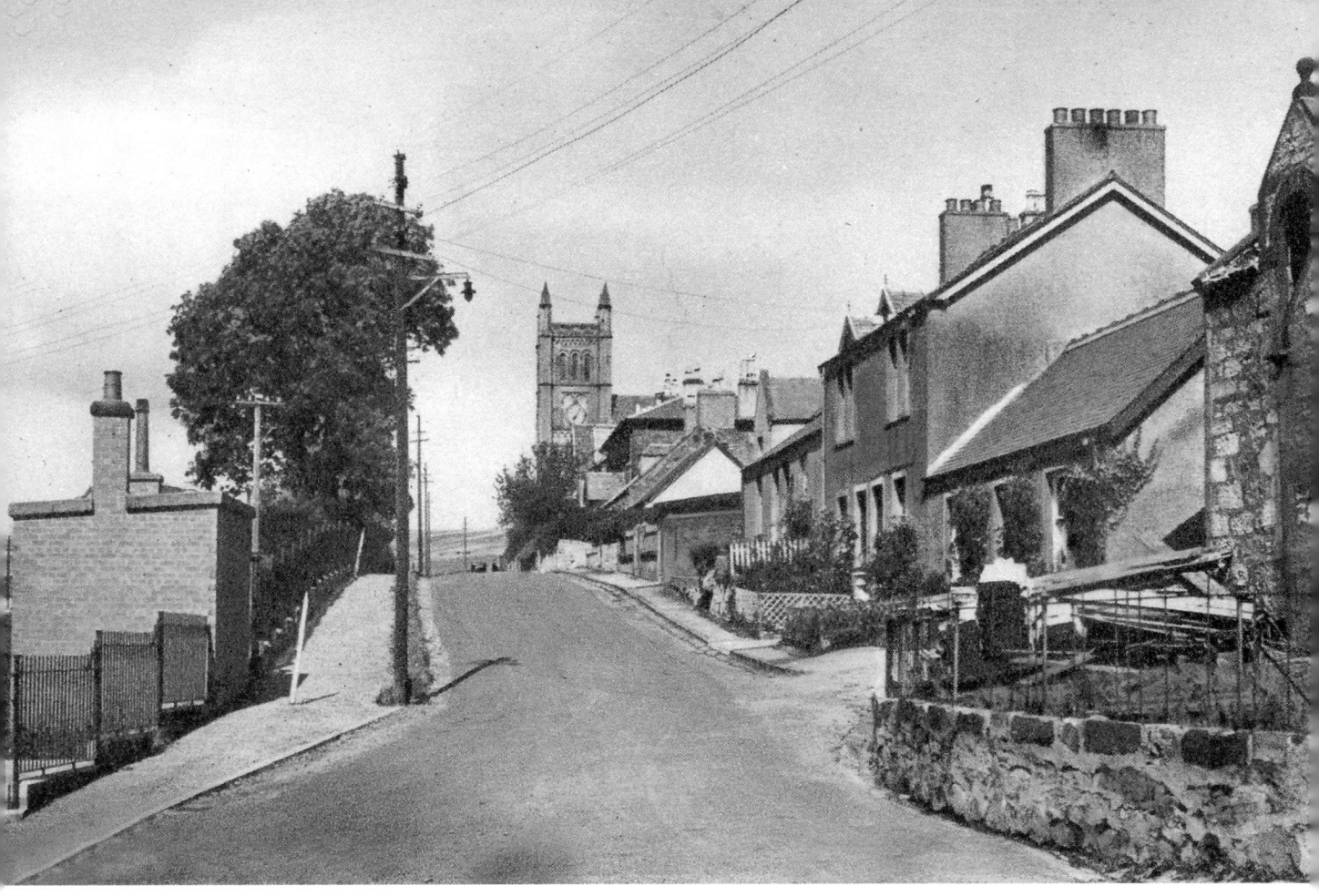

Knowehead

On older maps Knowehead is shown as Windy Raw, and it is still known locally by this name. The roadway, although much of a backwater in Dalmellington today, has an ancient history, for at one time this was part of an ancient route that made its way from Ayr into Galloway. Early maps show a so-called Roman road passing through Dalmellington, and this road formed part of the route.

At the right hand side of the picture is the church hall, originally the parish church itself from 1766. It is claimed that the church was built by James Armour, the father-in-law of Robert Burns. When it was erected, this would have formed a prominent corner position in the village. Writing in 1837, Rev Robert Houston complained that the church, 'though of no great age, from the dampness of the site … is exceedingly uncomfortable, and for both comfort and accommodation, it is ripe for rebuilding.' As the MacAdam Cathcarts had presented the new church to the parish, the old one became the property of Colonel Augustus Cathcart. He converted the building into a lodging house, much in demand with the construction of the ironworks and the arrival of many travelling workers. The house was so well thought of that it is said that when many Irish immigrants landed at the Broomielaw in Glasgow, they asked, 'What way is it to the old kirk of Dalmellington?'

In 1887 Colonel Augustus Cathcart presented the building back to the parish church, and it was subsequently converted into the church hall. The minister, Rev George Hendrie, published *The Parish of Dalmellington: its History, Antiquities and Objects of Interest* as part of the fundraising. The building was used by many church and other groups throughout the week, including the Temperance Association, Band of Hope, Women's Guild (formed 1894) and Young Men's Union. In 1898 the hall was used as a cinema, where films of the jubilee procession, Henley regatta and other events were shown. In this image, the church hall is shown as it appeared prior to 1938, when the architect Alexander Mair rebuilt it, removing the window gablets and arched windows.

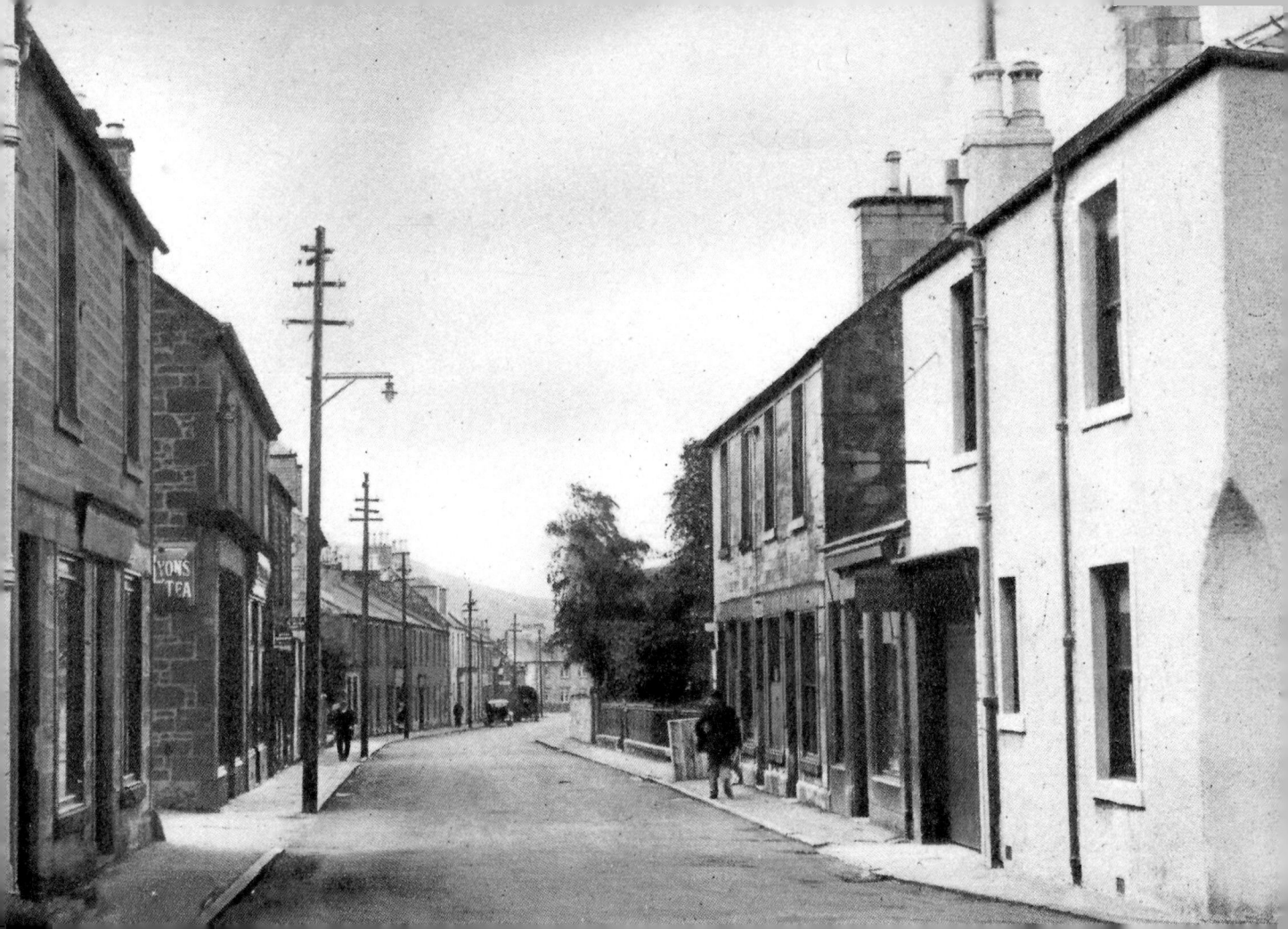

Main Street looking West

Main Street links the town centre with the road to Patna and Ayr. This early view shows the street looking west from near the top of Waterside Street. On the left is a shop that was occupied by John Clark & Son in the early twentieth century. This business operated as a drapers and milliners. By the second half of the twentieth century it was occupied by W. & M. Johnstone, a newsagent and stationers. At the start of the twenty first century it was occupied by Costcutter, a small grocery shop that also sold freezer food and rented videos. In more recent years it was the Newsplus store.

Beyond the lane is the present Keystore, but at the time of this picture it was occupied by Napier Brothers, grocers. One of the brothers was Peter Napier who lived in a house farther along the street, near to the Eglinton Hotel. On the right hand side of the street the white rough-cast building was owned by Alexander Gibson, game dealer. The chamfer on the building and the mark on the end wall was where some low cottages once stood, demolished to allow the erection of Gibson's Garage. The single-storey shop was Alexander Brown's fruit merchants and is currently Classic Cuts hairdressers. The double storey building that follows was at one time the location of the post office, which occupied these premises in the early part of the twentieth century. In the first decades of the twentieth century the shops were occupied by Thomas Wyllie, watchmaker, and George Cron, ironmonger. By the 1960s the far shop was occupied by John Trotter & Sons, drapers. In recent years, it was Rae the florists.

The railings and trees are located in front of the Royal Bank building, which sits back from the street. This was erected in 1875 to plans by Peddie & Kinnear, an Edinburgh architectural practice who designed many banks for the company. The bank opened its first office in the village in 1855 but did not become a full-time bank until 1879 when J. Walker was appointed as manager. The bank remained open until 2016.

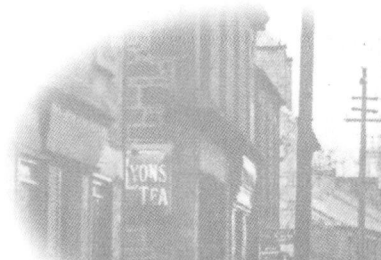

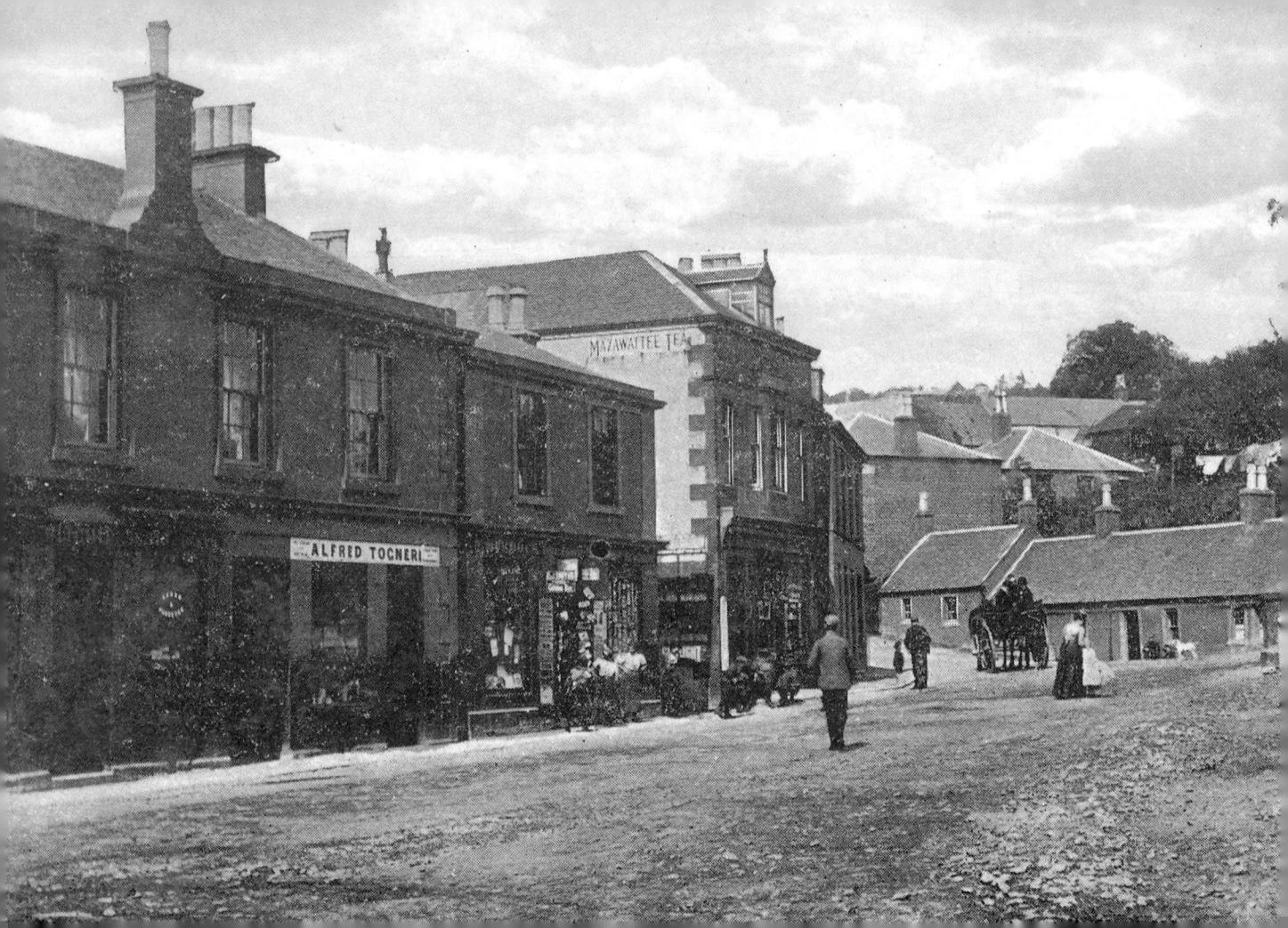

Main Street looking East

Taken from Main Street looking back towards the bridge-end, this old postcard view depicts the junction of Main Street with High Main Street. On the left is the building belonging to George Gibson (1850-1927), builder, with its distinctive eaves chimney. At the time the picture was taken, the shop on the left was occupied by the Bertillotti Brothers, ice cream dealers. Next door was the bakery of Ritchie Scott (1852-1913). The shop with the sign reading Alfred Togneri was a confectionery, and was previously occupied by the Bertillotti Brothers. It was also known as the Brig End Café and had a bakery owned by MacCallum. To the right in the adjoining building is William Murdoch's newsagent and tobacconist shop. Dalmellington's post office was located in this building for a time around 1890. On the far side of the close is William Ritchie Stewart's (d. 1935) grocery, with an advertisement for Mazawattee Tea painted high on the wall. William Stewart was a keen antiquarian.

To the right of the picture is a row of three cottages, part of High Main Street. Old photographs depict them with thatched roofs. The back windows faced onto the Muck Burn and on a number of occasions they were subject to some serious flooding. The water takes a sharp turn to the rear of the cottages, and when in spate it often came against the back walls. One of the last major floods to affect the cottages occurred on 11 July 1927 - the water in the Muck Burn was so high that it burst through the back doors and windows, flooded the houses, and poured from the houses through the doors and windows back into the Square. After this, the cottages were abandoned, and new buildings were erected on the site. To the right is the parapet of the Muck Burn Bridge. This dates the picture to before 1915, when the new steel-sided bridge was added at an angle slightly downstream, to aid traffic flow when the School of Aerial Gunnery was being constructed at Loch Doon.

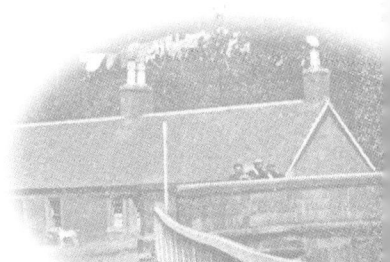

A Look Back at DALMELLINGTON ~ *page 15*

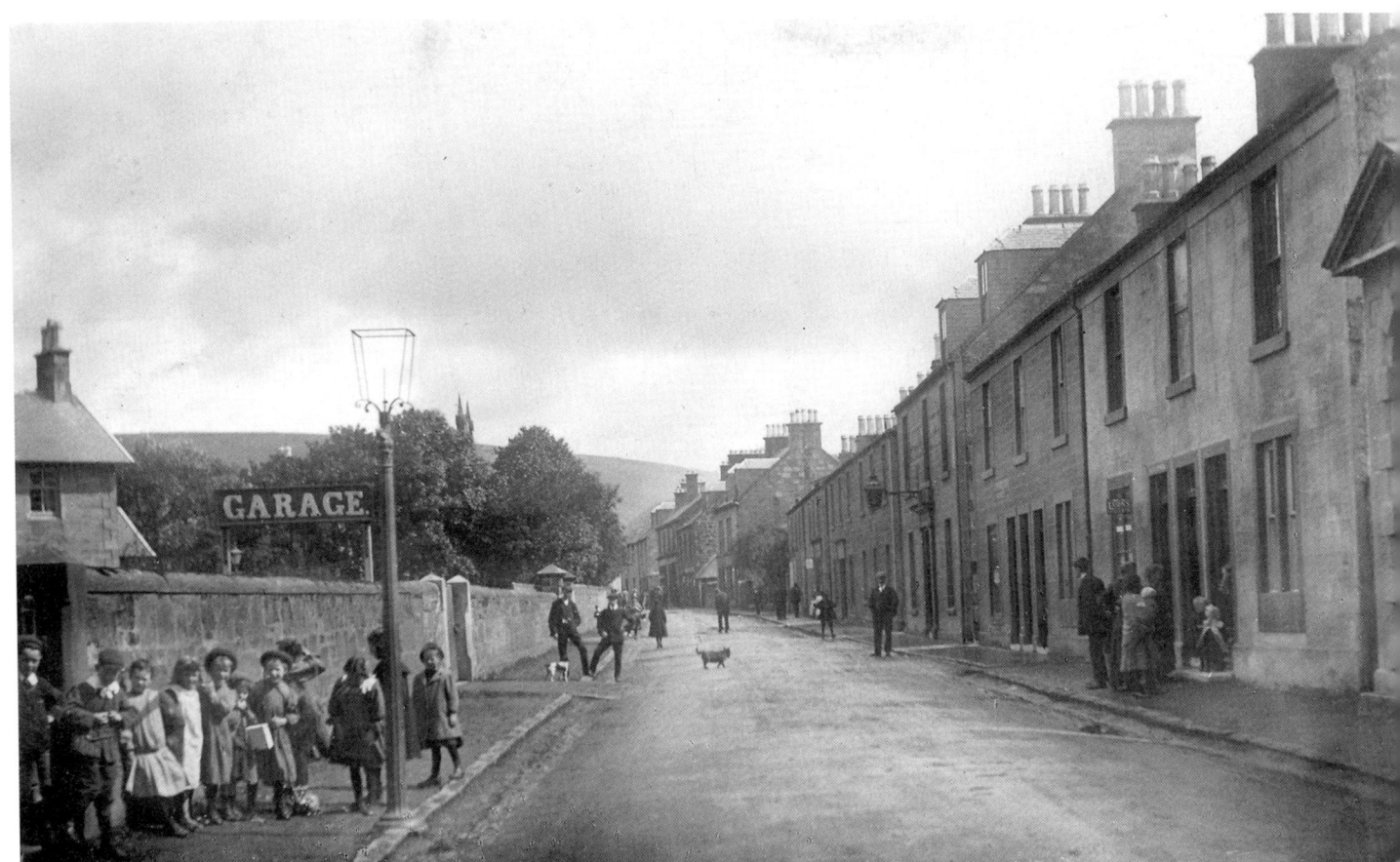

Low Main Street

Taken from the western end of Low Main Street, near its junction with Ayr Road, this view shows a busy thoroughfare – busy at least with pedestrians and onlookers. The building on the immediate right of the picture was Our Lady of the Rosary Roman Catholic Church. This was opened on 7 October 1860 by Bishop Murdoch. There were only one or two Roman Catholic families in Dalmellington in the early nineteenth century, but with the erection of the nearby ironworks and the influx of Irish workers, their numbers grew considerably. Originally, they were served by priests from Ayr, and services were held in the Black Bull Hotel hall. Initial plans for a church at Waterside didn't come to fruition, and eventually the old Morrisonian Congregational Church in Dalmellington was acquired and the chapel erected on the site.

The Catholics had to endure much persecution in the early days, and some folk were wont to shout abuse into the chapel during services. This apparently stopped when Thomas Prendergast, who had been positioned near the door, caught one of the culprits and punched him! Priests who served here were Hugh Gallagher (1862-79), William Dawson (1879-80), Frederick Letters (1880-88), Daniel Kerrin (1888-91) and John Fouhy (1891-95), after which date the chapel was closed when the new chapel at Waterside was opened.

Next door are two tenement buildings, the second one now being home to Lodge St Thomas No. 433. The building was acquired by them in 1965 and after years of renovations was opened as a masonic temple on 7 April 1971. The building with the projecting lamp standard is the Eglinton Arms Inn. In the early 1920s the proprietor was John Clark, and there one could hire three boats on Loch Doon at five shillings per day each. At a later date, when James MacDonald was proprietor, an advert for the hotel stated that it was 'recently enlarged, renovated and refurbished at considerable expense, and the latest sanitary improvements introduced'. There were 'airy bedrooms', a 'billiards saloon', and now the hotel had 'eight good boats (three of them new) with careful and experienced boatmen on Loch Doon'.

A Look Back at DALMELLINGTON ~ *page 17*

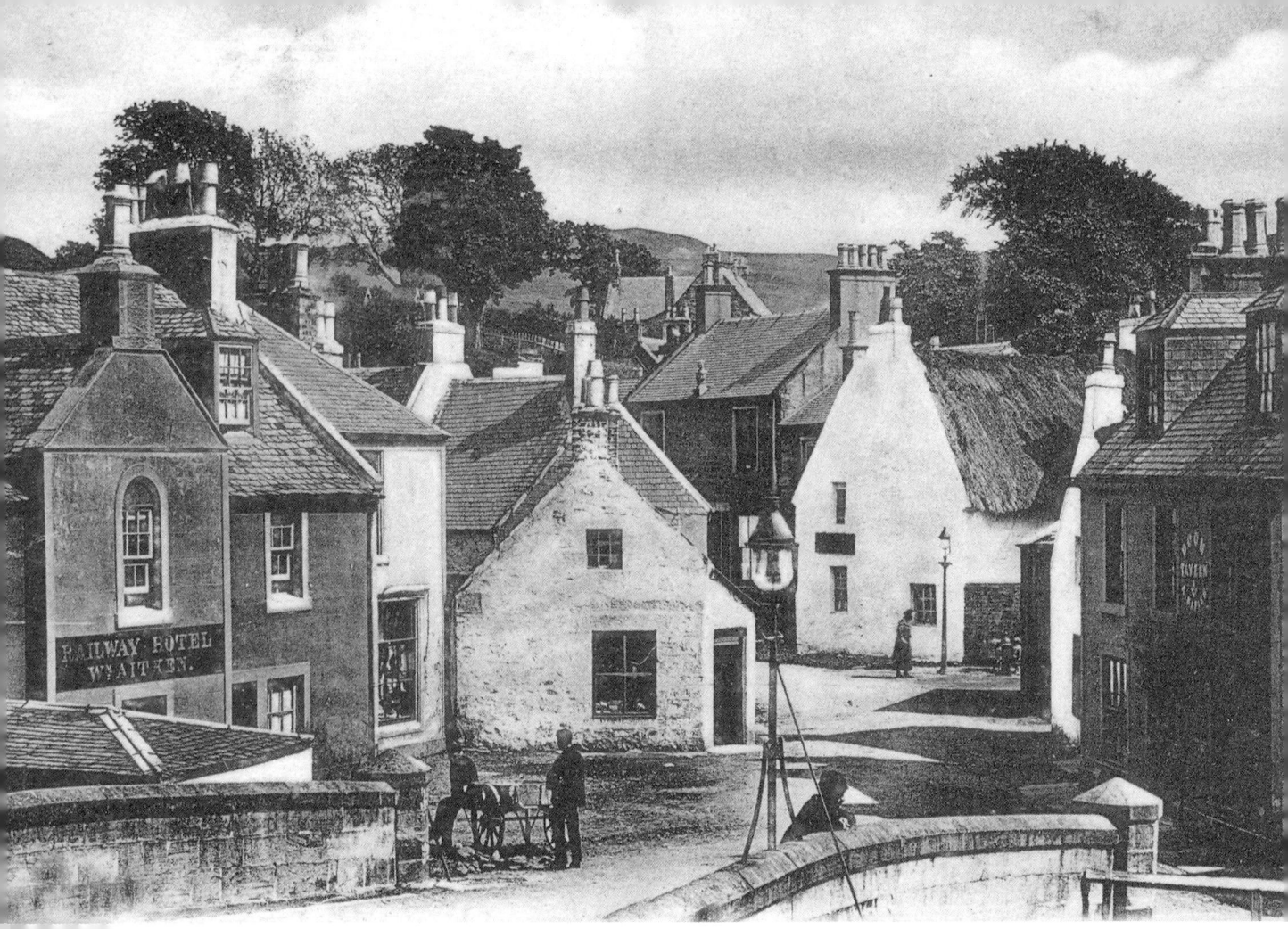

Two Old Inns

The Railway Hotel takes its name from the arrival of the railway into Dalmellington, which took place in 1856. The main reason a line was built to the village was more to export coal and iron, rather than any great demand by passenger numbers. Nevertheless, the station was constructed at the western end of the village, on open ground at what was the extremity of Main Street. The Railway Hotel was distant from the station, but to those visitors coming from afar, it would appear to be next to it, and the inn would gain custom in this way. Previously, it was known as the Craigengillan Inn. The building dates from the early nineteenth century, with a projecting gable at the main entrance. Proprietors over the years include Gilbert Carmichael (around the 1860s), William Aitken (c. 1900), and William Dodds (1914). The inn was later renamed the Dalmellington Inn. In recent years the rendered walls have been stripped back to reveal the natural rubble stone. When the bridge was widened the low roofed part in front of the inn was removed.

On the opposite side of the street from the Railway Hotel is the Doon Tavern, another of Dalmellington's hostelries. This was established as an inn in 1876, once the Royal Bank vacated the premises. When the picture was taken the proprietor was Alexander Napier. He was succeeded by James Napier. In more recent years the proprietrix was Mary Dey. In the distance, to the right of the lamp standard, is a water pump, a source of water for the residents. Behind the pump and lamp is a double-storey thatched house. This was one of the older buildings in Dalmellington, and bore the name Castle House.

The small building with its gable facing the photographer and the doorway on the angled corner was the original post office. In 1850s and 1860s the postmaster was Robert Smith. Letters arrived at the office at quarter past eight each morning, and were despatched therefrom at half past one in the afternoon. Smith also acted as agent for the North British Insurance Company.

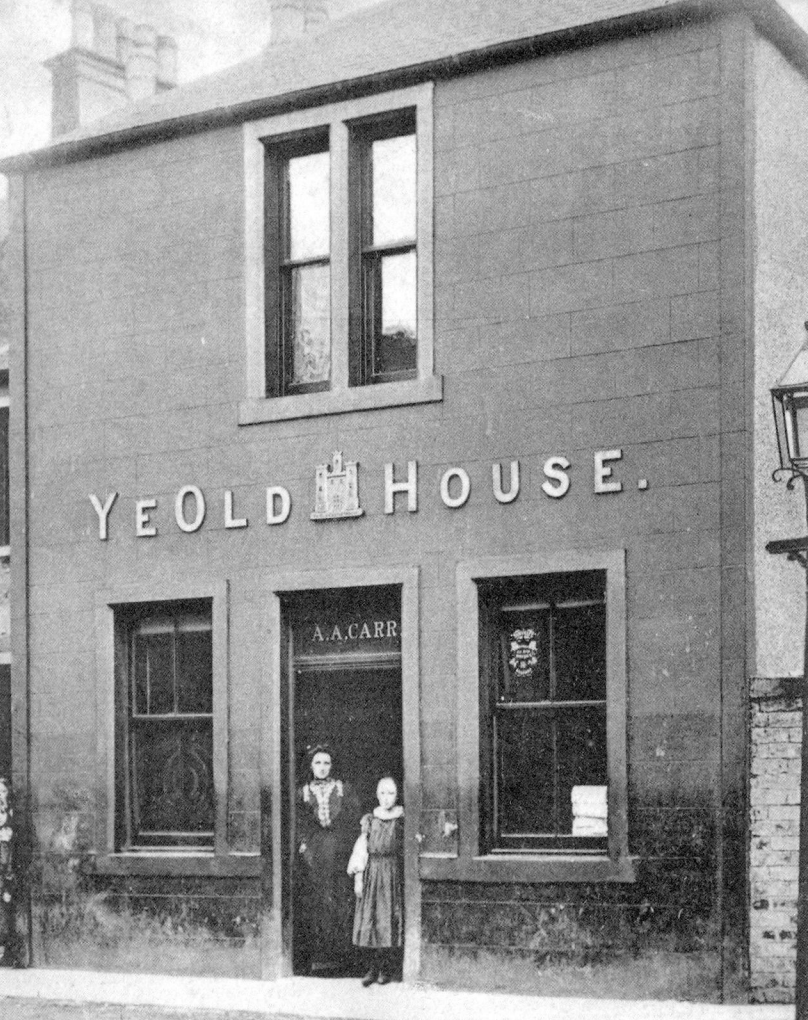

Ye Old Castle House

The thatched Castle House building in the previous view of High Street was rebuilt in the early 1900s when a hipped slate roof was erected over raised walls, built of brick but covered over with smooth render. On the façade, 'Ye Old Castle House' was made out in letters, the word castle being represented by a carved building. The building received its name from the tradition that it had been erected using stone taken from Dame Helen's Castle, a ruin located further up the New Road.

According to the *New Statistical Account*, written in 1837, there was a date stone of '1003' visible on Ye Old Castle House in 1800, but such tales are usually mistakes for dates in the 1600s, which is more in keeping with the style of the original building! James Paterson, writing in 1847, saw this lintel, but as far as he was concerned it read '1115', and Rev George Hendrie, writing in 1889, claims that he heard a third date for the stone. The building is certainly of a considerable age, for the ground floor to the rear of the building has a stone vaulted ceiling, that room originally containing the kitchen.

When this image was taken the building was used as a public bar, the proprietor being Albert A. Carr (1865-1920). He rented the building from Elizabeth and Janet N. MacWhirter, who acquired the inn in 1898 from Mrs Gerrand. Carr was the bandmaster of Dalmellington Silver Band from 1888 until 1910. Carr was a Yorkshireman and on his appointment to the band moved to Dalmellington from Merseyside. He was given a job working in Pennyvenie No. 2 pit, but later became a publican. He lived at Poole Cottage, which was located in a lane behind the Dalmellington Inn. He and his wife, Susan, were to lose three sons during their lifetime. They are buried in the parish cemetery. The bar was latterly used as an agency of the Newcastle Building Society. In 2015 the property was acquired by Scott Brown and work began on renovating the building into a private house.

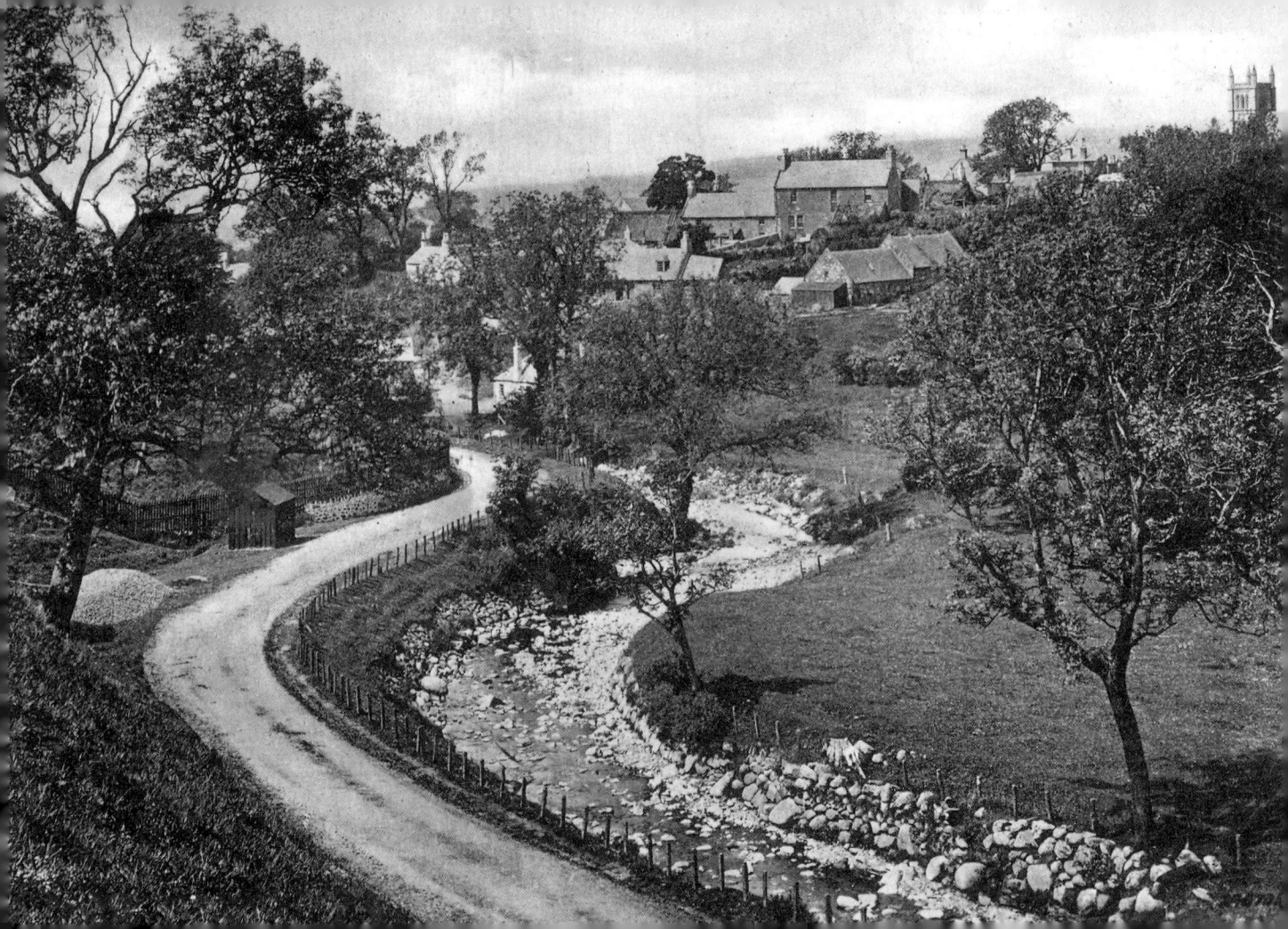

New Road

The New Road was built in the early 1800s to provide a wider and less steep route out of Dalmellington heading south, compared with the narrow climb of Townhead, followed by the moorland track over the Town's Common and Pennyarthur Rigg. This old roadway was often regarded as being of Roman origin, but modern historians dismiss this, its wandering route being unlike the straight Roman roads constructed elsewhere.

New Road was built alongside the Muck Water, seen to the right of the road. It joined Carsphairn Road at the Kirnbridge Toll Bar. It was laid out at the time Mr Woodburn, father of Dr Woodburn, was the estate factor. On the horizon to the right is the tower of the parish church. The back of the houses in Church Hill are seen to its left. The large house is Sean Baile, or Church Hill House, which is thought to be one of the oldest surviving houses in the village. On a rear wall is a date stone of 1638, though the present building may be from the following century.

In front of Sean Baile is the old corn mill, which was powered by water from a lade diverted from the Muck. Not seen in the picture was an old waulk mill, used for fulling cloth, which was probably demolished by the time this picture was taken. It was located to the front of the corn mill. The lade also drove the wheels of a third mill before returning to the Muck, just short of the footbridge at the foot of The Path. This was a spinning mill. On the right of the image, where the tree with the light-coloured bark is, was the site of an earlier mill. This had long-since disappeared by the early nineteenth century. On the centre left of the picture is an area fenced off with a wooden picket fence. This area is the ancient motte hill, partially hidden to the left by the large tree. By the side of New Road is a wooden hut, and an area around it, where once was the Mote Well, a local source of fresh water.

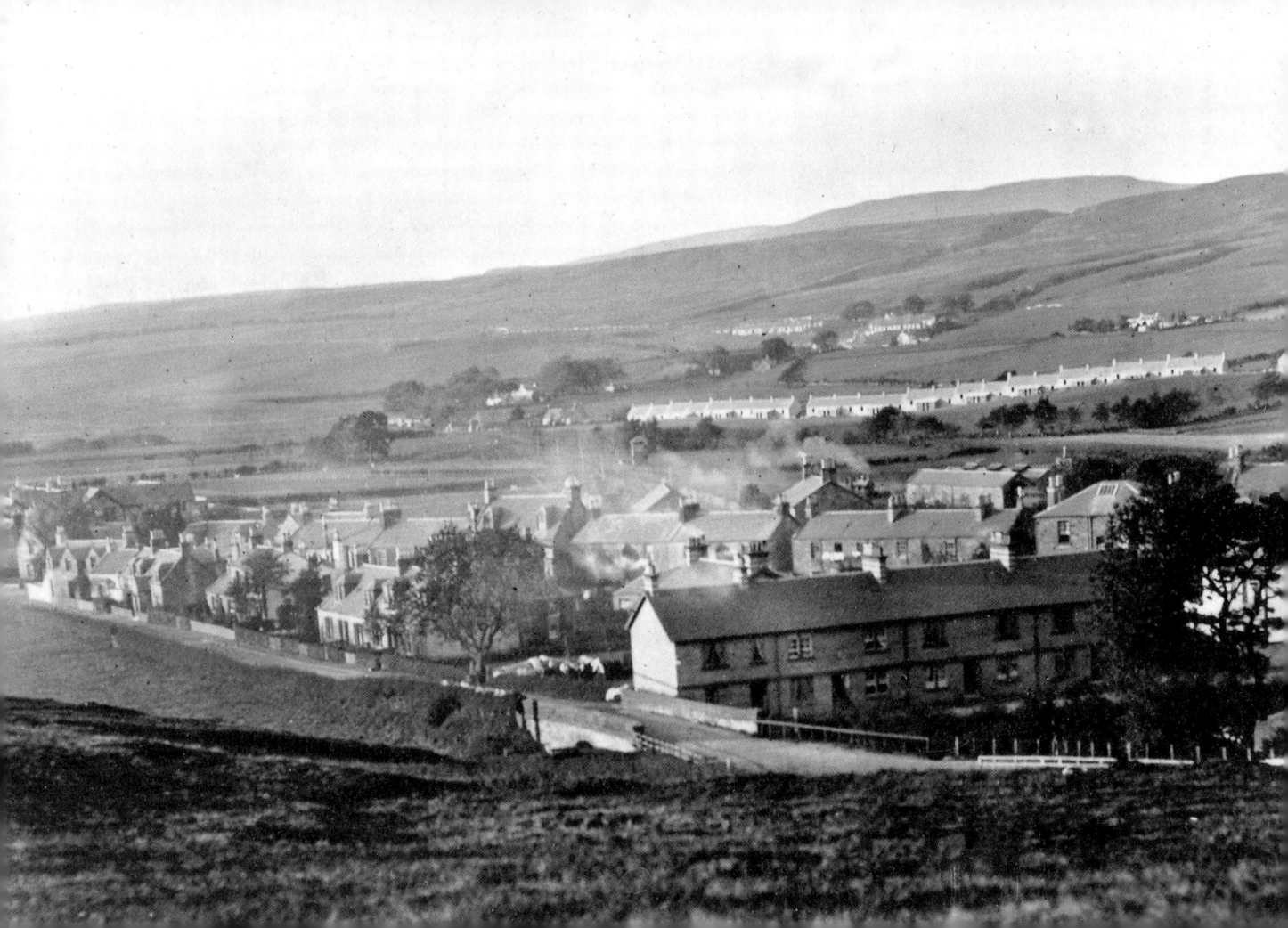

Bellsbank Road from the East

Taken from near Cockie Knowe, this view depicts Bellsbank Road on the left, at the time of the picture only built up on the northern side. Most of the houses in this street were erected in the late 1800s or early 1900s. At the time of the picture there were only eight houses in the street. Nearest the photographer was a terrace of four cottages. This comprised Rosebank and three other houses, originally owned by William Murray and John Bain. Murray's properties were let to James Napier, spirit merchant, and William Ireland, joiner. Bain's properties were let to William Smith Bain and Alexander Bain, drapers. The semi-detached cottage (Lucknow) obscured by the next tree was also owned by John Bain, who lived in one half, the other let to Thomas Ness, chemist.

At the eastern end, facing onto Waterside Street, is a tenement block known as Knoweview, comprising of 22 brick-built houses accessed from four closes. This block was erected in 1903 by the Dalmellington Iron Company, the first houses to be erected by it within Dalmellington itself. For a time, the building became known locally as Rory's Den. The houses were noted for their lack of amenities and within a fairly short period had degenerated into what was described as 'near slums'. It was later demolished and Knoweview House nursing home was erected on the site, opening in October 1991. This has 60 bedrooms for residential care.

In the middle distance can be seen the long line of miners' houses, built at Broomknowe, on Gateside Road. Forty houses were erected in 1910-12 and were far superior to many other miners' rows of the previous century. Built of bricks manufactured at Dunaskin Brickworks, the houses were also erected by the Dalmellington Iron Company. These houses were regarded as 'model' homes when they were erected, even although they had an outside toilet. In the far distance, in the fold of the hills, can be seen the houses of Craigmark, an old mining community that has long-since been cleared away. The houses there were erected in 1845, or thereabouts.

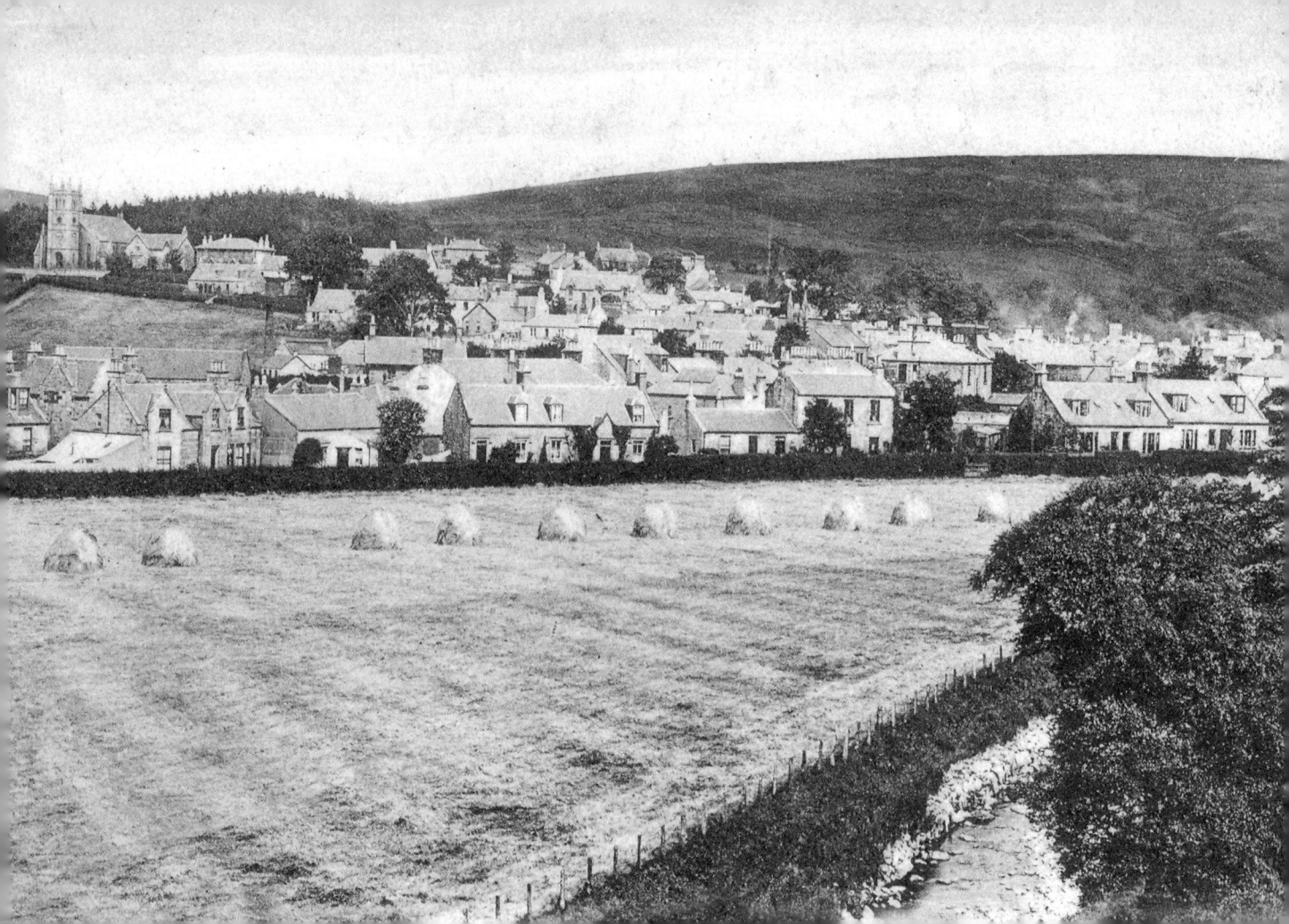

Bellsbank Road from the West

Taken from an elevated embankment at the southern side of the Muck Water, this picture looks across the hay meadow, where now Bellsbank Crescent is located, towards Bellsbank Road. The date is around 1900. At the right-hand end of the road is a short terrace of four houses with dormer windows, known as Rosebank. To the left of this are two buildings joined together, the double-storey house being home of John Bain (1832-1919), clothier. John Bain & Sons, drapers, were located in a shop next to the Eglinton Hotel in Main Street and the business had been established in 1856. The houses would have been erected in what was originally the back gardens of the Main Street buildings, but with the opening of Bellsbank Road a new frontage meant that development took place in the back gardens. The shop was taken over by William Smith Bain (1867-1951) whose son, John Johnstone Bain was killed in action in France in 1917. The business was closed down sometime before 1935. John Bain owned a number of cottages and houses in the village, including some at Knowehead and The Path.

Next again to the left is a pair of cottages which were originally owned by William Ireland, farmer at Burnton and West Chalmerston. At the time of the First World War, these were occupied by William Smith, tailor (to left) and James S. Porteous, teacher (with porch). The building between the tree and a bush was the former Roman Catholic school, and to its right, on Main Street, was the chapel. The school and the building to its left have been demolished and the site forms a wider entrance to Low Main Street.

The field in the foreground was to be where Bellsbank Crescent and other houses in Bellsbank Road were erected in 1929. The four homes in one cottage-style block were typical of thousands erected by Ayr County Council across the county, principally to rehouse families from sub-standard homes. A total of forty homes were erected on the hay field shown, the first residents coming from condemned miners' rows.

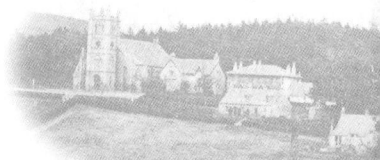

A Look Back at DALMELLINGTON ~ *page 27*

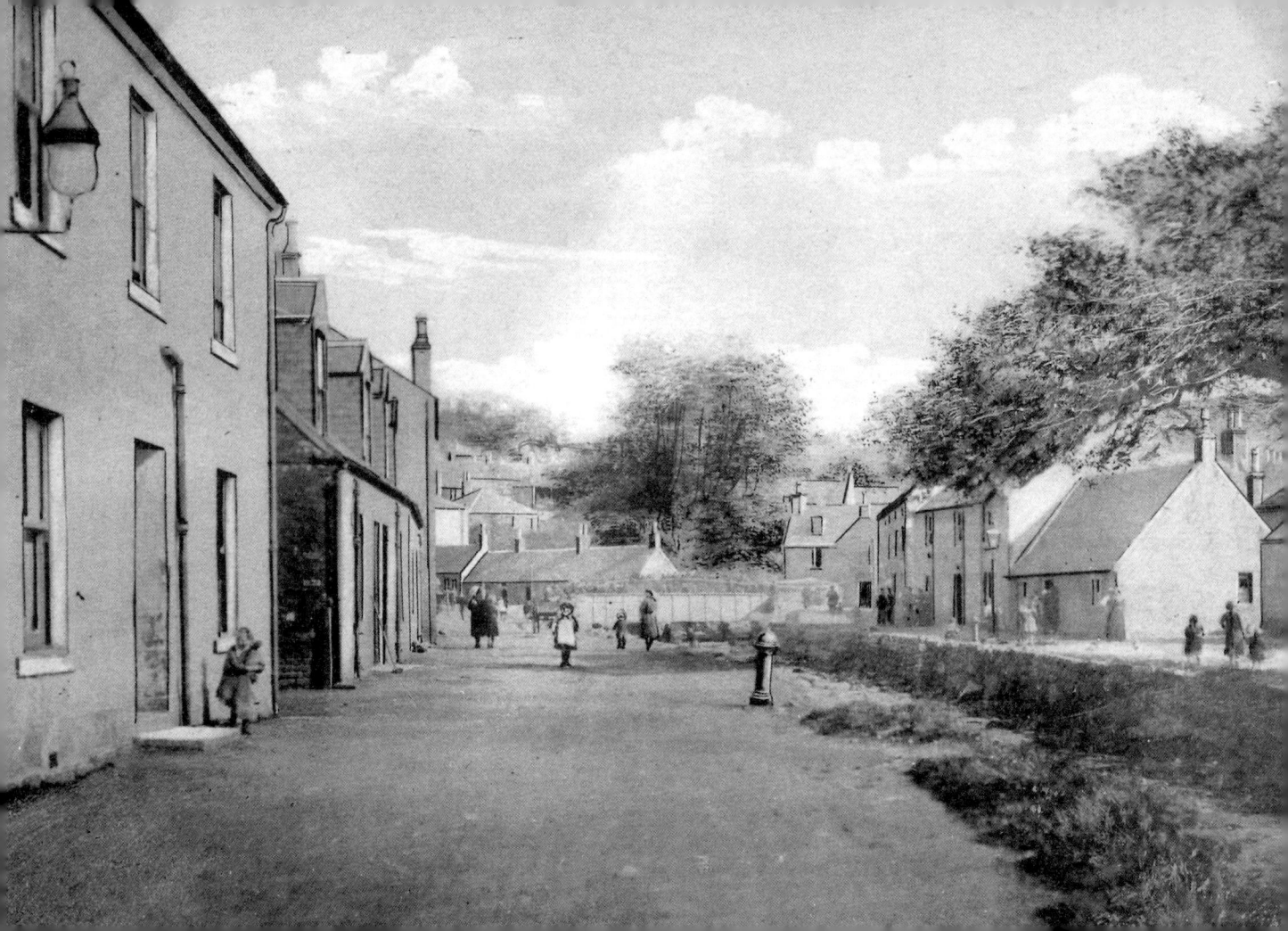

Waterside Street

When this postcard was published, Waterside Street was referred to as Burnside Street. On the left is an old building that dates from before 1855. The single storey row beyond, with the dormer windows, is newer, having been built in the garden of houses in Low Main Street. A water pump is located by the waterside. Around 1886 the first real water scheme for supplying Dalmellington was inaugurated. This comprised of an intake on the Mossdale Burn followed by a filter and tank, with a water main into the village. Demand for water grew and a second intake was constructed, on the Trough Burn, with an upgrading of the pipes. In 1906 this was again extended, and a small reservoir on Mossdale Burn was formed in the late 1920s. Water pumps, manufactured in Kilmarnock by Glenfield, were located at the bottom of Main Street, in High Street, opposite Lamloch Church, at the top of the Gas Brae, half way along Knowehead, and at Cathcartston, in addition to this one. Not seen in the picture is the old school, located to the photographer's left-hand side.

On the east side of the Muck Water is Cathcartston, a street of buildings facing onto the burn. Cathcartston is named after the local landowners who developed this part of the village – the Cathcarts of Berbeth. In the gap at the white gable is New Street, a name that has been in existence since before 1850. In Cathcartston was a Bethany Hall. One of the buildings in the row starting behind the large tree has a date stone of 1744 and the initials AMC. The house was converted into a museum in 1985, originally known as Cathcartston Interpretation centre, but was renamed the Doon Valley Museum.

In the centre of the picture can be seen the iron bridge across the Muck Water. This was erected in 1915 when the Loch Doon School of Aerial Gunnery was being constructed as part of the war effort. This proved to be a total disaster, the cost of which was never revealed. The bridge was replaced in 1935 when the present concrete bridge was built.

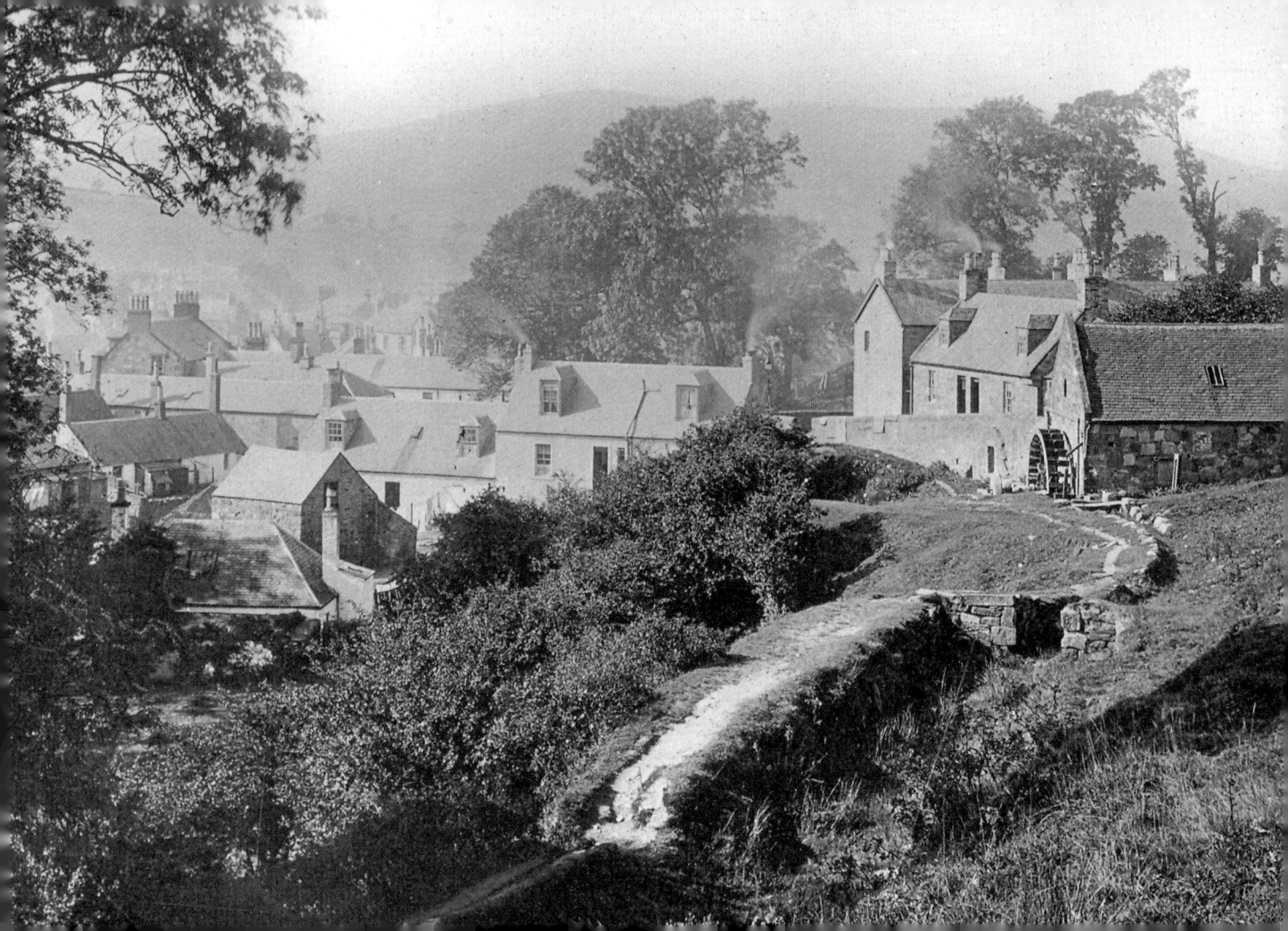

Dalmellington Mill

This old postcard shows the mill which was located just off The Path. The lade, which supplied the waterwheel with water, is seen in the foreground, long-since dried up. The stone wall indicates where the final sluice was, the unwanted water being diverted back into the Muck at this point. The water in the lade was captured from the Muck Water, which was dammed beneath Dame Helen's Castle. A sluice controlled the flow at that point, and the Miller's Burn passed along the Miller's Bank to the mill, a distance of around half a mile. The water turned the mill-wheel, here visible, but in the picture on page 22 it is covered in, before dropping quickly to the left and returning to the Muck. Only around eight or ten feet of head of water was utilized, and if the mill had been located nearer the Muck then a head of almost thirty feet could have been used.

The waterwheel was of a breast paddle type, around two feet six inches wide. It has been calculated that the wheel would have produced around six to seven horse power. Within the mill building itself were two millstones, driven directly from the waterwheel by means of cast iron gears and shafts. The stones were of the Kaimshill type, having been brought here from a quarry on the hill above Fairlie at the north end of the county. The mill was one of the older buildings in the village, erected to grind corn, and originally was the barony mill. This meant that everyone in the Barony of Dalmellington had to have their corn ground there. The barony was owned by the Wallaces of Sundrum Castle in the fourteenth century, but passed to the Cathcarts. The mill was latterly part of Camlarg estate.

Among the millers known to have ground the corn here were William Arthur (1782-1853), who was buried in the old kirkyard, and James Bell (miller in 1868). By the Second World War the mill had been abandoned and the mill stones were lying outside. The mill has since been demolished.

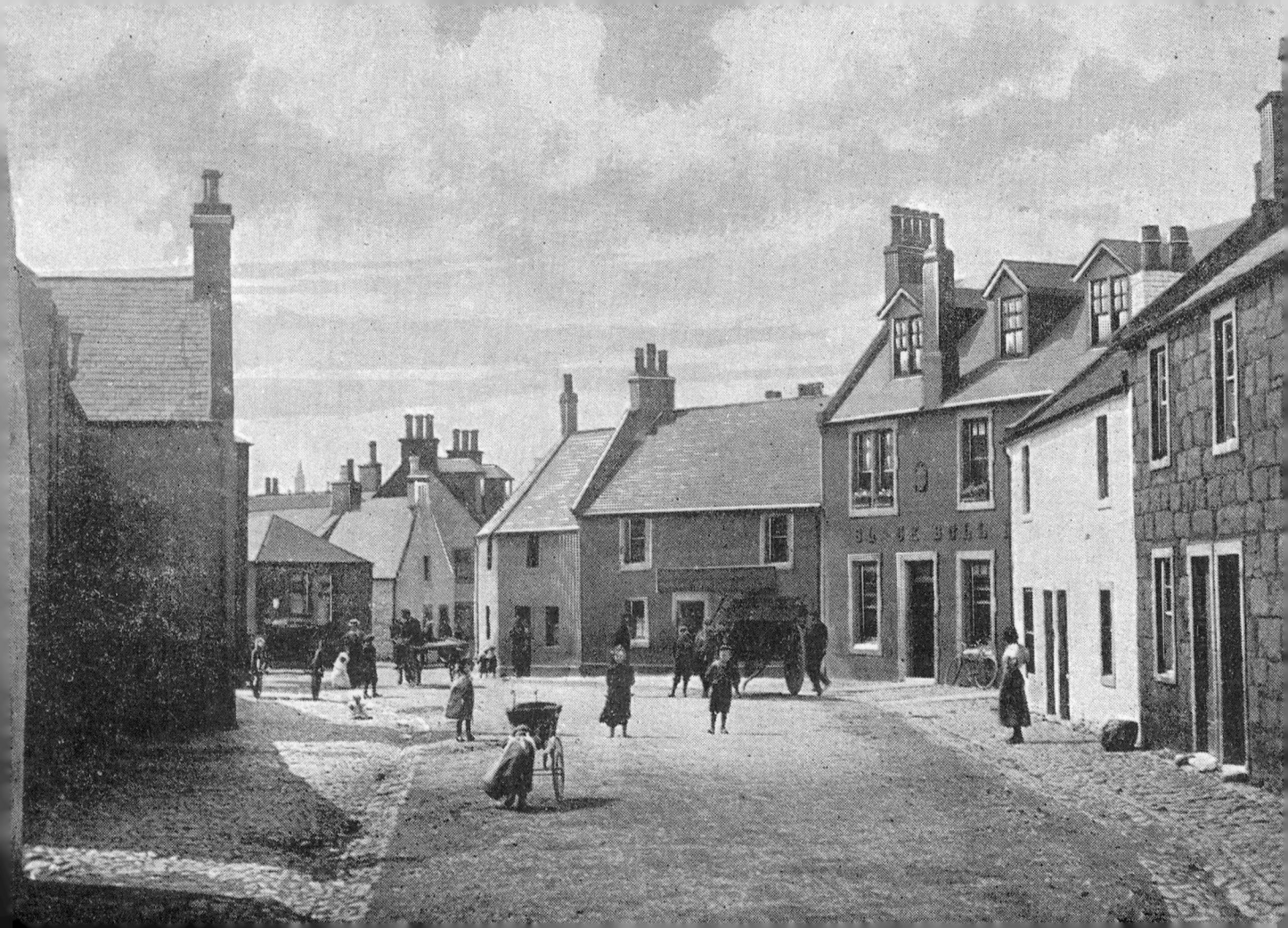

High Street looking West

Looking westwards along High Street, this picture was taken around 1900. On the right is Midton Cottage, which some folk claim is the oldest surviving building in Dalmellington. Built into the wall adjoining the left-hand door is a carved stone depicting masonic emblems. On an outbuilding is a date stone inscribed 1744. It is claimed that John Graham of Claverhouse, the persecutor of the Covenanters, stayed at Midton Cottage whilst searching for the hill-folk in the district. Two residents of the village, George MacAdam, merchant, and Thomas Sloss, were taken prisoner and held in Edinburgh for a long time. The Earl of Dumbarton and an army of 6,000 militia camped at Dalmellington in 1685 for three weeks, searching for Covenanters. When he moved on he is said to have left a gibbet as a warning to the locals.

Next is the Black Bull Hotel, an old hostelry that was erected in the early 1800s. In 1851 the landlord was Duncan Wight, followed by James MacCulloch (1827-1863). On his death his widow, Marion MacMurtrie took over, marrying James Broadfoot. She died in 1867. In the late 1800s the host was J. Coats, and in the early twentieth century it was Agnes Park. It was rebuilt in 1894-5 to plans by Allan Stevenson of Ayr. This view shows the hotel soon after that work was completed, with the addition of the carved date stone over the door, dormer windows in the roof, and the tall wall-head chimney. It was renamed the Loch Doon Hotel and in the 1960s was run by H. E. Westfield.

The bar next door was demolished in the 1950s and a new Snug Bar was erected on the site in 1958. This was built by the brewery firm, Maclays of Alloa, their thistle logo being displayed on the wall. In 2015 the bar was converted into a house. On the left hand side of the picture, the south side of the street, is the building that was formerly the Cross Keys Inn. The lane between it and the gable nearest the photographer led to the smithy.

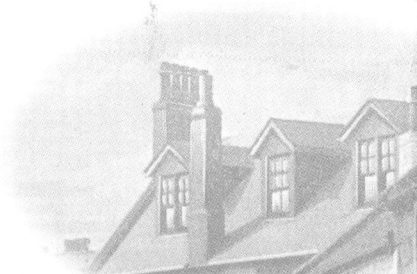

A Look Back at DALMELLINGTON ~ *page 33*

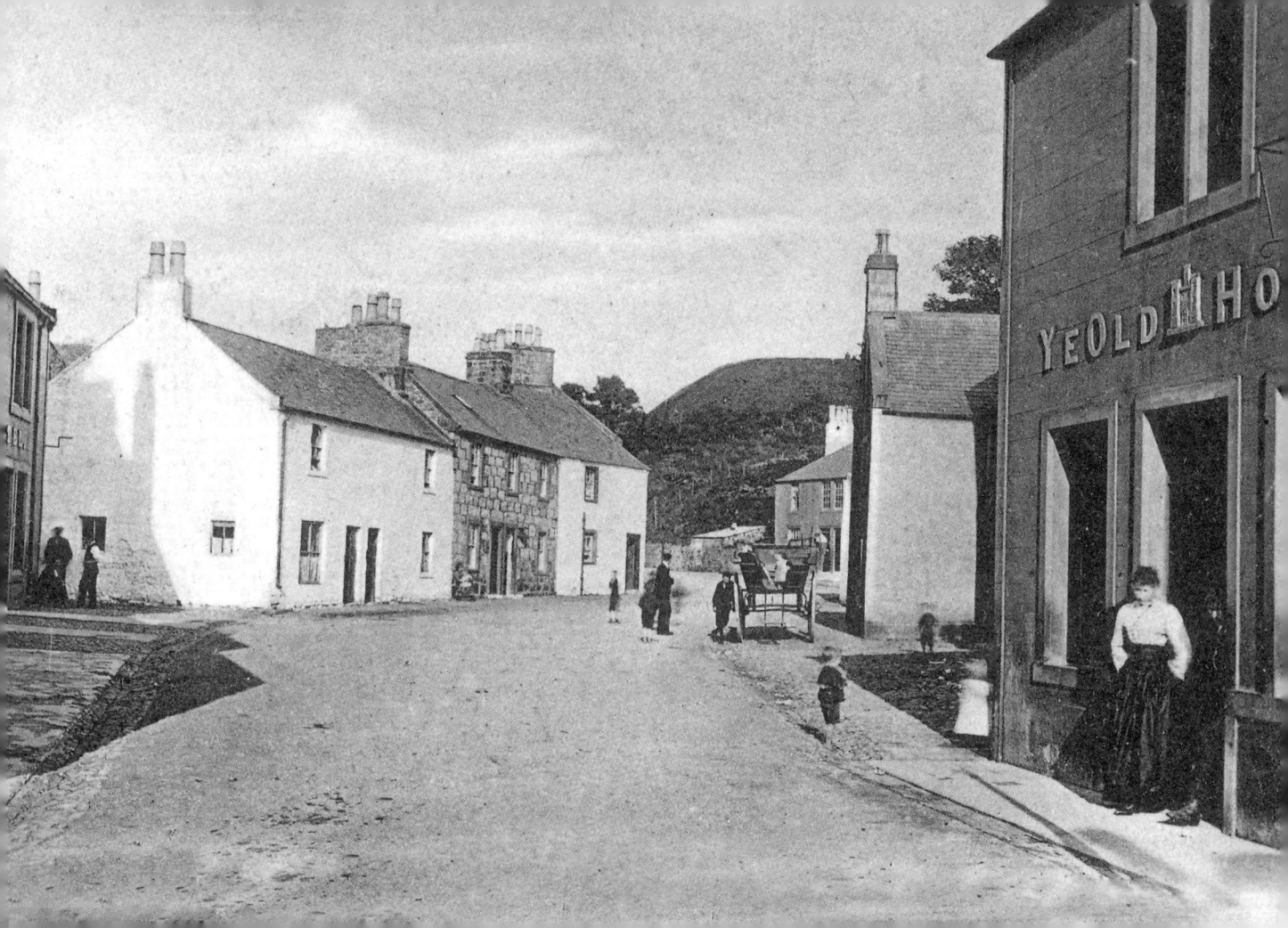

High Street looking to the Motte

An old picture of High Street looking eastwards. Outside Ye Old Castle House can be seen a gas lamp standard. The gas works in Dalmellington were originally located at the top of Townhead, hence the street being better known as the 'Gas Brae'. The gas works were later to be relocated to Croft Street.

The next building on the right, with a gable facing the street, was the Cross Keys Inn. An old coaching establishment, in 1837 it was run by William Sloss. He also had the lease of the local coal mine at Camlarg. This worked coal seams 120 feet below the ground. These were 22 inches and 36 inches thick, the coal selling for three shillings per ton. The inn became the property of Alexander Baird by 1867 and he offered fishermen boats for hire on Loch Doon. In 1896 the inn became the masonic lodge for Lodge St Thomas. This was founded on 1 April 1864. The lodge bought the inn for £150 and following fundraising and renovations to the building, it was consecrated on 21 October 1899 by Brother Matthew Arthur. The building has recently been demolished.

Between the Cross Keys and Ye Old Castle House is a house known as Dr Alexander Jamieson's House. This was where the celebrated doctor (1798-1826) was born. His bust is located on top of the eaves, facing the street. Dr Jamieson was also something of a poet. The present building is dated 1861. At the far end of the street can be seen the motte hill. Mottes were usually constructed in the twelfth and thirteenth centuries as places of defence. They would have had a timber palisade and buildings within them. Dalmellington's motte is one of the finest in Ayrshire.

At the last building on the left side of the street was a branch of the Edinburgh & Glasgow Bank in the mid nineteenth century. Midton House next door has the bare stone frontage. To the left of the central white house is a lane which leads to a footbridge across the Muck Water and thence to Churchhill by way of the Path.

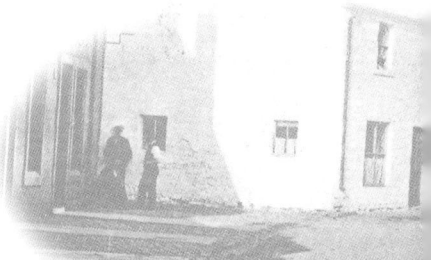

A Look Back at DALMELLINGTON ~ *page 35*

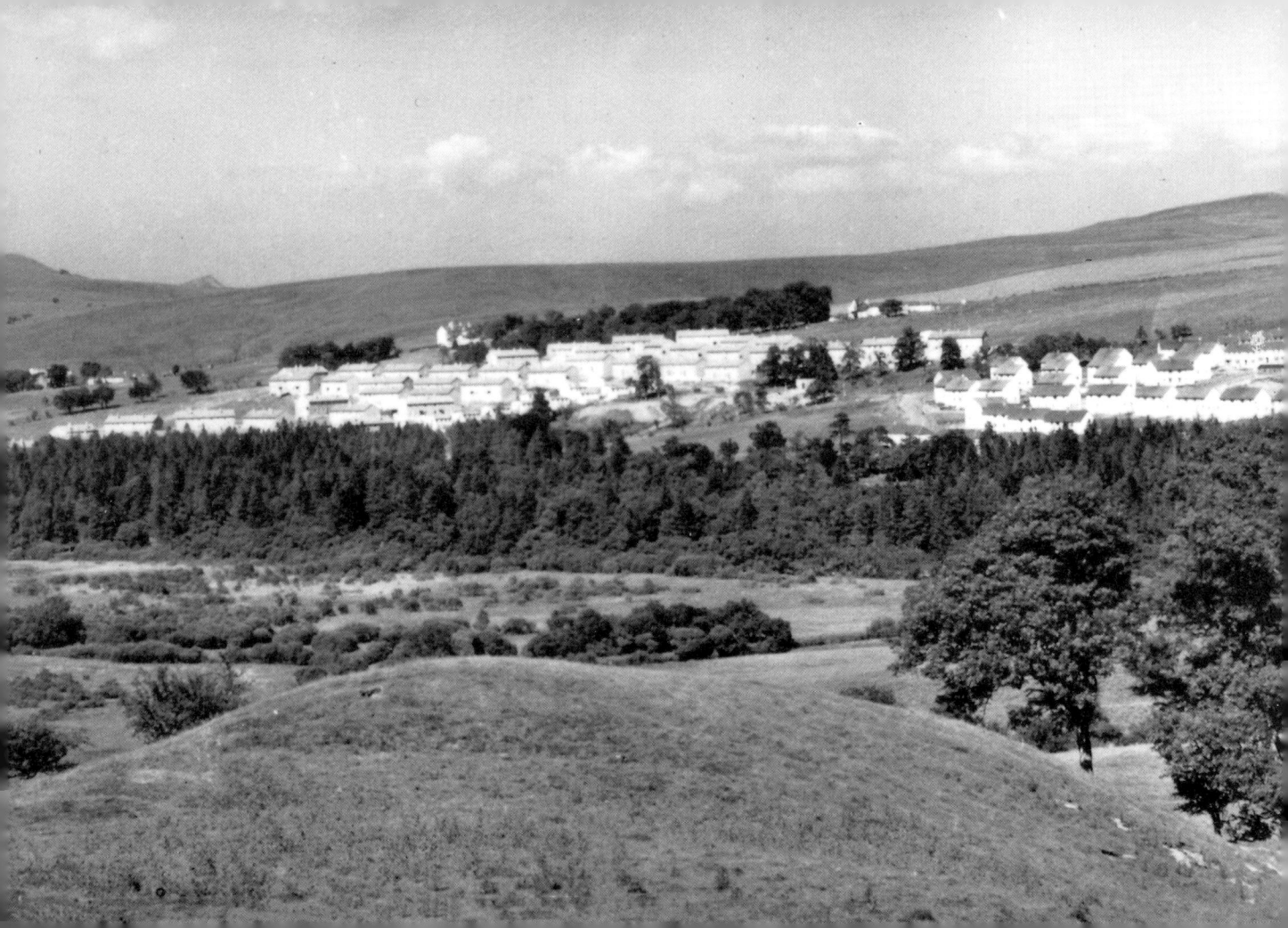

Bellsbank

The old miners' houses that were in Craigmark, Pennyvenie and other communities became unfit for habitation in the mid twentieth century. The National Coal Board began a programme of building new houses to rehouse the families who lived in the old rows, and Bellsbank was one of the larger communities created in the Doon valley. The scheme was completed by Ayr County Council. Located south of Dalmellington, and accessible by a single road, most of the houses had two or three apartments over two storeys. Some houses, such as those in parts of Dalcairney Road, were prefabricated single-storey houses.

The streets were named after local places, such as hills (Corserine Terrace, Minnoch Road, Merrick Drive and Craiglea Crescent), lochs (Finlas Avenue, Macaterick Drive, Bradan Avenue), farms past and present (Mossdale Terrace, Eriff Road, Dalfarson Avenue, Auchenroy Crescent), or local scenic spots (Ness Glen Road, Dalcairney Road). The new community was supplied with a number of shops and commercial premises, including a post office.

Bellsbank Primary School was opened in 1955. The roll was in excess of 300 at one time, but it had fallen to 83 in 2016. A new school building incorporating an early learning centre is being planned. A church building was erected in 1956-7, as an extension charge of Lamloch Church in Dalmellington. The church was dedicated on 2 April 1958 by Very Rev Professor J. Pitt-Watson DD. The Lamloch Church was fully united with the church at Bellsbank in 1974 and the former was closed. In 1983 the Lamloch church was united with Dalmellington Parish Church.

The adventure playground at Bellsbank was launched in 1985. In recent years the number of people wishing to live in the district has fallen, and many houses in Bellsbank are no longer required. Subsequently, many houses were demolished, including the prefabs in 1976, plus 80 homes in Dalcairney Road, Finlas Avenue and Auchenroy Crescent in 1994 and 46 houses in Mossdale Terrace in 2011. Others have gone in Corserine Terrace and Dalfarson Avenue. This postcard view shows Bellsbank from the west, looking over the River Doon from Tod Knowes.

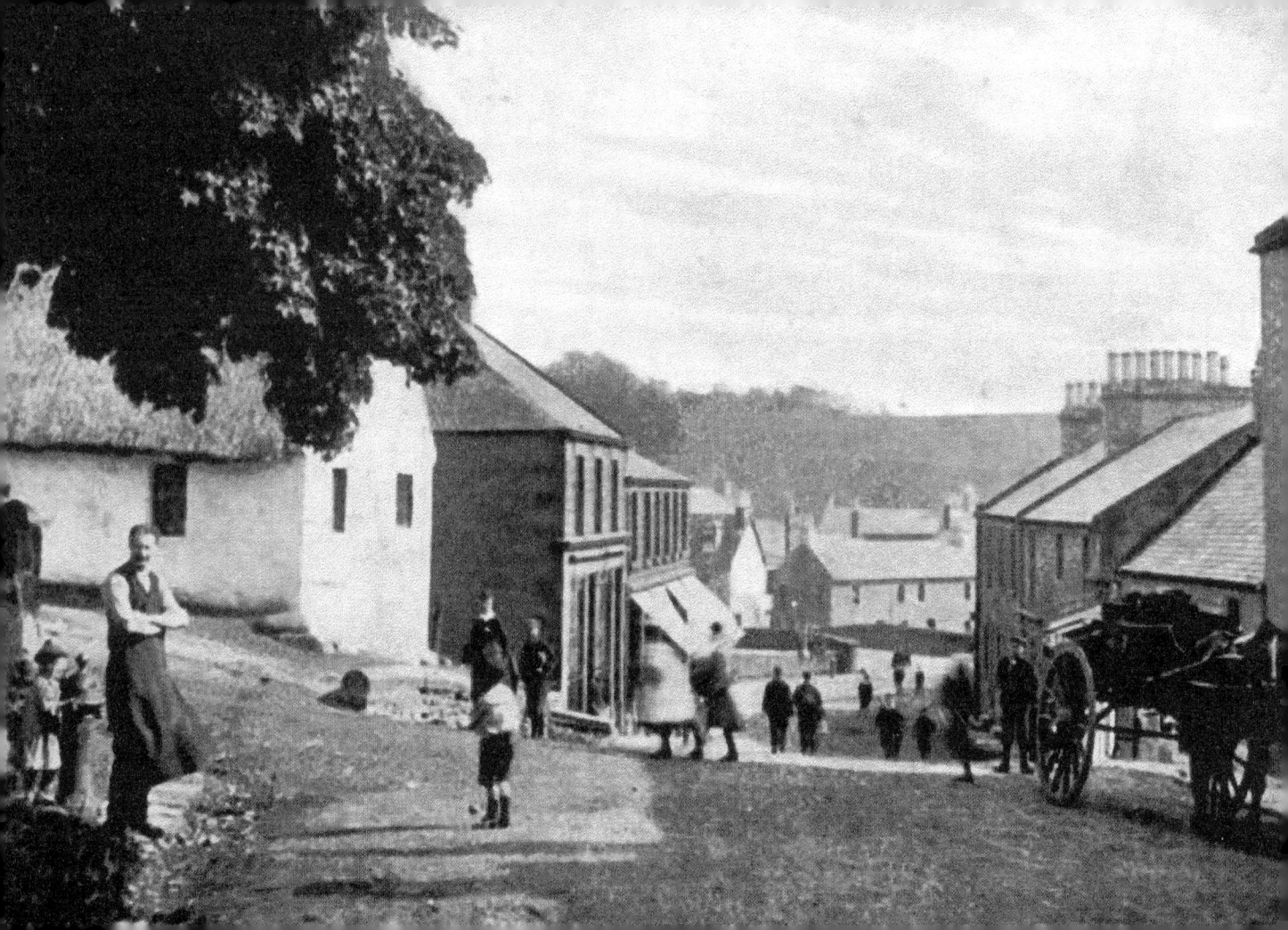

High Main Street

This view depicts High Main Street, looking downhill towards the cross. On the left is the start of Churchhill, known at that time as Church Street, the thatched cottage typical of much of early Dalmellington. Behind it are the premises of Dalmellington Industrial Co-operative Society Ltd. On the opposite side of the street the double storey building at the bottom of the hill was the co-op boot and shoe shop. It was later occupied by George Fyfe's chemist shop, latterly taken over by Hay the chemist. The building with the lower roof was Wilson's grocery and confectionary in the 1960s.

In High Main Street lived Robert Hettrick (1769-1849), the 'blacksmith poet'. He wrote many verses on local topics. His 'Poems and Songs' were collected together in 1902 and published by the parish minister, Rev George Hendrie. At the bottom of the right hand side of the street was Gaa's Reading Room. This was established in 1835 when John Gaa (1757-1834), shopkeeper in the village, left money in his will to found a reading room. The shop was left to the trust also, the rent used to support the library, which in 1836 had 600 books.

Gaa stipulated that 'there is no person to be a member of that Reading Room but what are of good morals nor is any drunkard to be admitted as a member. Each member must pay something when he enters as what is given for nothing is not thought worth receiving". Any profit was handed over to assist in educating the poor. In 1896 the trustees handed over the rooms to the parish council. A fund-raising scheme was organised which raised £100, allowing more books to be purchased, bringing the total to almost 2,000 volumes in 1901. In addition to the reading room, two recreation rooms were added, the whole being renamed Gaa's Institute. The reading room remained the village library until a new building was erected at the bottom of Townhead in 1982, designed by Roy Maitland of Cumnock & Doon Valley. The library was closed in 2016 and is now the Dalmellington Carers' Centre.

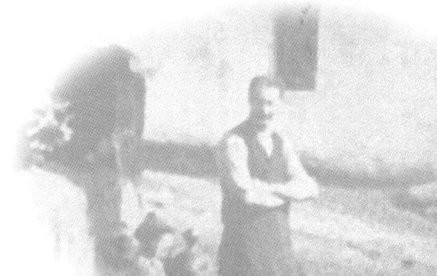

A Look Back at DALMELLINGTON ~ *page 39*

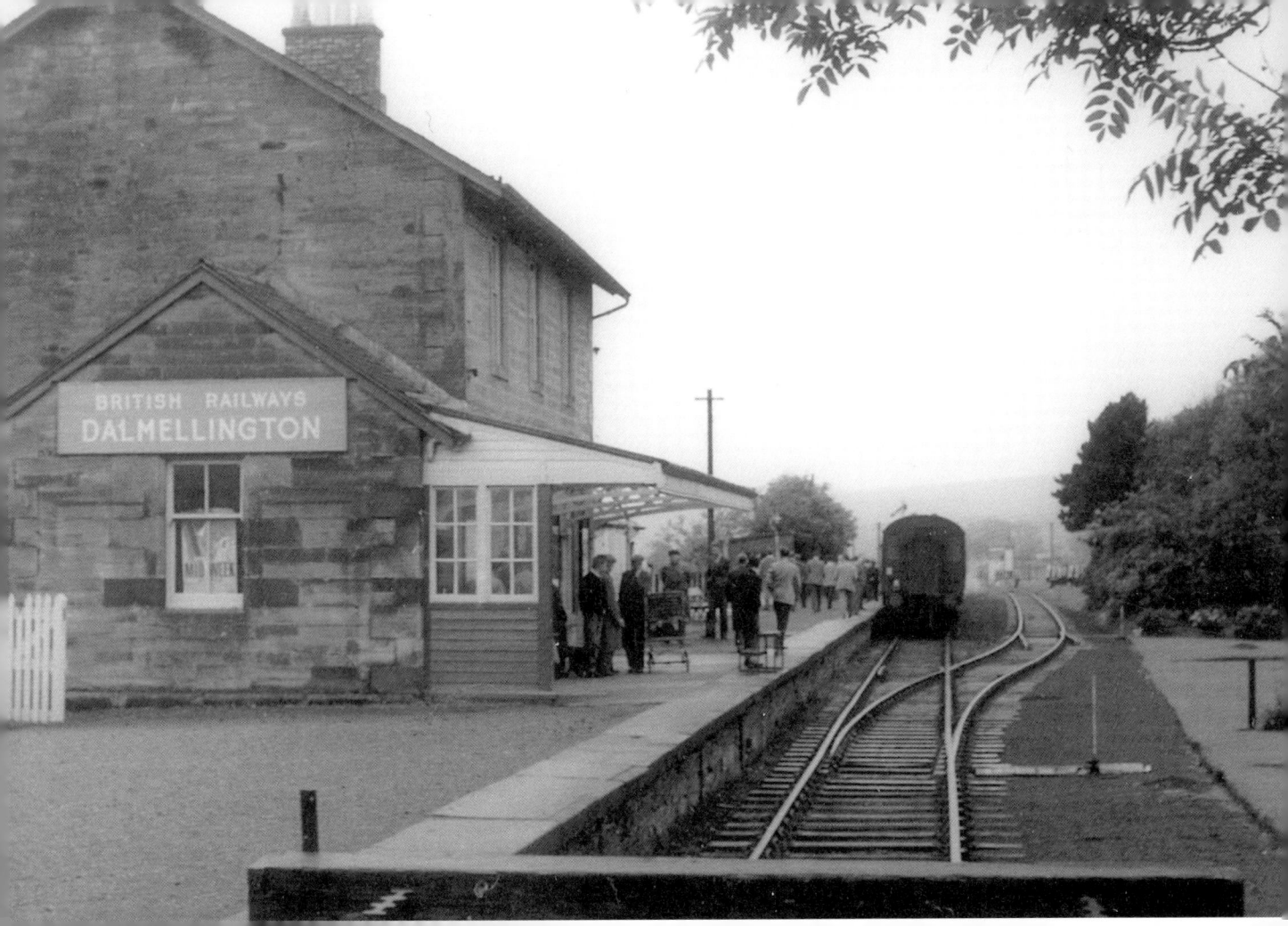

Dalmellington Station

The railway arrived in Dalmellington in the mid nineteenth century. In 1846 the Ayrshire & Galloway Railway Company proposed a line through Dalmellington to Balcary Bay on the Solway Firth, where a port was proposed. This came to nought. The Ayr & Dalmellington Railway Act was authorised by parliament on 4 August 1853. The line was laid by the company soon after and it reached its terminus at the village, where a station was created by the side of Low Main Street. The line was opened firstly for goods traffic on 15 May 1856 and the station was opened to the public on 7 August 1856.

The Ayr & Dalmellington Railway became wholly vested in the Glasgow & South Western Railway on 1 August 1858. Before the First World War there were five passenger trains arriving in Dalmellington daily. By 1937, to compete with the growing bus services, there were twelve trains per day, for a period powered by Sentinel steam railcars. After the Second World War there were only three services per day. In 1948 the railway was nationalised, and various services were experimented with, including running every ninety minutes and running a three-car diesel unit.

By the late 1950s, services had again been reduced to two trains per day, with an extra one on Saturday. At one time there was a large engine shed nearby, and a turntable, where engines could be turned in the opposite direction. This appears to have been removed around 1932, after the railway was taken over by the London Midland and Scottish Railway in 1923. The Dalmellington branch line was closed to passengers on 6 April 1964, after which the rails at the station were lifted. The last train to leave the station was a three-car diesel unit, driven by George MacNeil of Ayr.

The site of the station was developed as a small industrial area. This was later to be converted into a council office, with police station, health centre and dentist. This view is taken from the final buffer on the line, looking north-west. On the left is the station building and behind the trees was the engine shed.

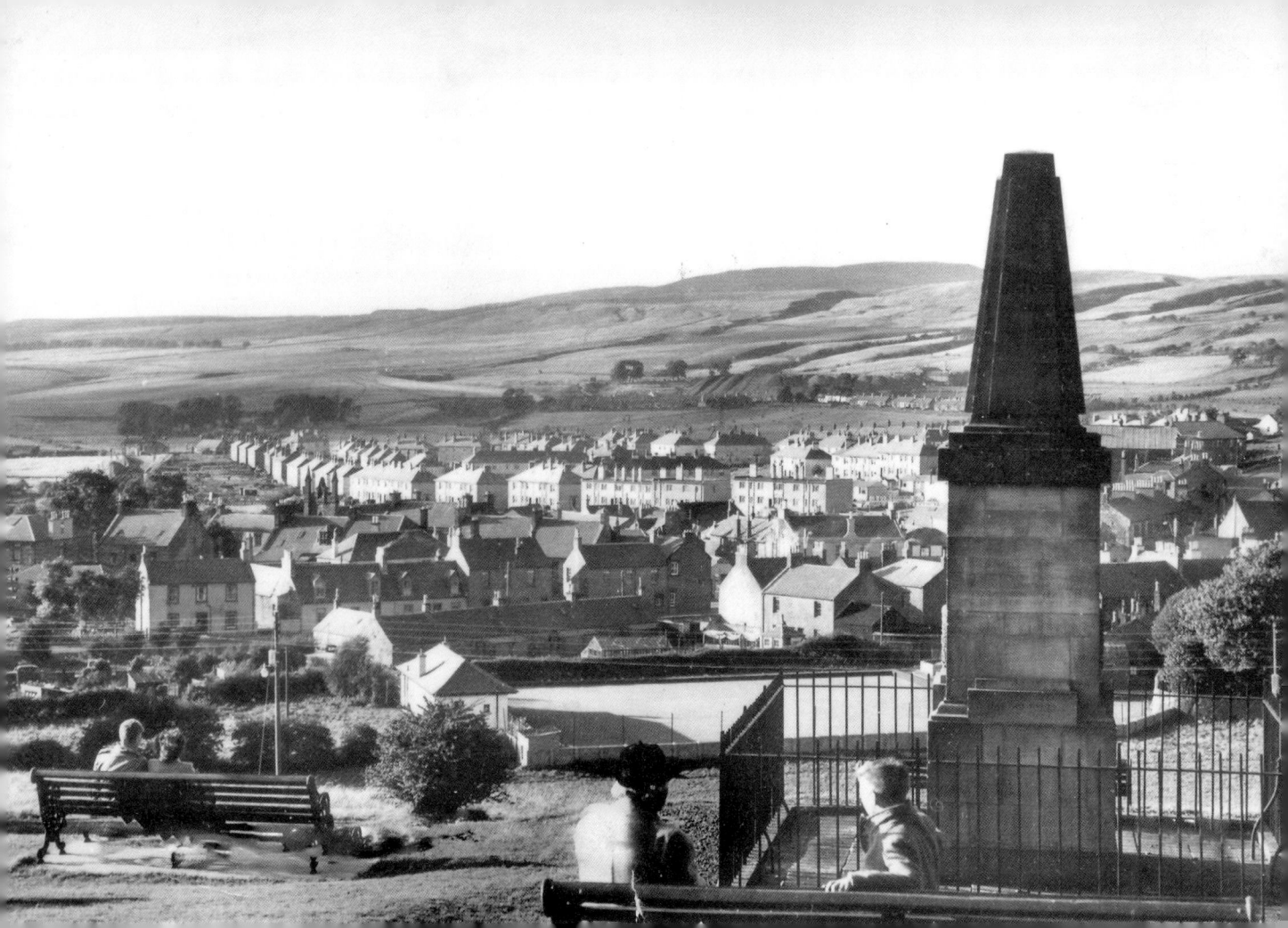

War Memorial

Following the resumption of peace at armistice, after the First World War, the thoughts of the locals turned to forming some form of permanent memorial to all of those who lost their lives in the conflict. At first it was proposed to erect a War Memorial Hall and Recreation Rooms. Plans for an elaborate H shaped building were drawn up by Stevenson & Cassels, architects, of 14 Cathcart Street, Ayr. However, it was soon realised that the cost of this was more than had been raised. An alternative plan to raise a war memorial was pursued, and eventually the new monument was unveiled on Sunday 16 April 1922 at 3:00pm by Mrs James Stewart, who had lost three sons in the war, and Mrs George Cron, who lost two.

The memorial was located on an elevated position off Bellsbank Road, as seen in this postcard view. The sculptor was James Scott Glass of London - he was selected as he was a native of the village. The stone obelisk is made from Cullaloe stone. On one side was a bronze panel sculpted by J. L. Emms, however this was removed in a recent renovation. The war memorial lists 108 men from the parish who were killed in the First World War. The list includes John Blair Cook, English master at Dalmellington School. At a later date a further 31 names were added of men killed in the Second World War.

The view from the memorial looks over the village, and the houses in Waterside Street are easy to identify beyond the bowling green. Also prominent are the council houses in Parks Crescent and Hopes Avenue. The miners' houses at Burnton can be picked out behind the memorial.

A memorial to the local mineworkers was erected adjoining the war memorial in 1996, just at the end of Cumnock and Doon Valley District Council. The memorial was unveiled on Sunday 31 March 1996. Sculpted by Patna monumental sculptor, Kevin Roberts, it depicts a Davey safety lamp and the inscription, "It well recalls the triumphs past." Dedicated to the mineworkers of the Doon valley.'

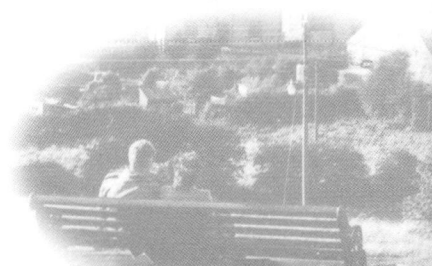

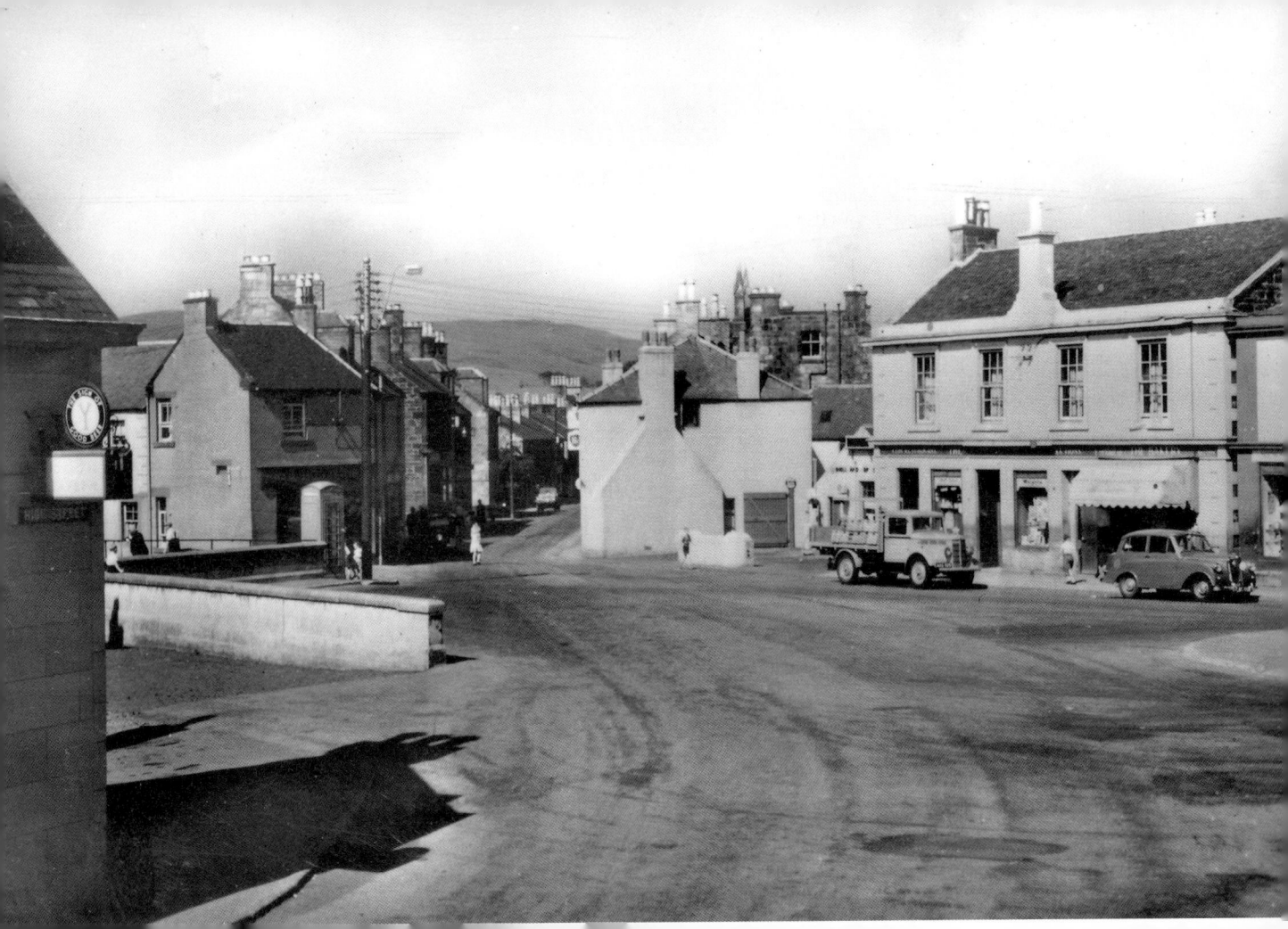

Square looking West

This image dates from the 1960s and shows the centre of Dalmellington looking over the bridge from High Street towards Low Main Street. On the left of the picture is the Doon Tavern. This building was originally erected as a branch of the Royal Bank of Scotland, the agent for many years being Robert Guthrie (1799-1879). When the bank moved to new purpose-built premises in Low Main Street this was converted into a public house.

Rev George Hendrie, writing in 1902, suggested that 'the present stone structure may be removed and the burn covered over by means of iron girders and plates. If this could be accomplished from the site of the present bridge to the first house on the west burn side, we should have a square in the middle of the little town that would give it much more appearance.' The bridge was rebuilt in 1935-6, extending it downstream and creating a large roundabout at the junction of the various streets. The work was held up due to inclement weather, and the new culvert could allow around 25% more water to pass through. The construction work was carried out by Kings and Co. Ltd. of Glasgow. The new bridge was tested in floods in 1937, when it was reported that it coped adequately. However, in 1939 much of Cathcartston and Main Street were flooded in an August rainstorm.

On the immediate right is S. Maguire's newsagents. Previously the shop was run by David Brown, and before that by William Murdoch, who published various books on Dalmellington, and some early postcards. To its left, with the sunshade out, is MacCallum's bakery. The lorry itself belonged to John Robertson of Patna, who ran a successful dairy business at the time and delivered milk across the Doon valley. The end of Croft Street has Gibson's garage, which sold Shell and BP oils and fuel. On the opposite side of Low Main Street, behind the telephone box, was Malcolm Ross's butchery. He ran this business from the 1920s until around 1965. It was then taken over by James Paterson, followed by his son, William Paterson.

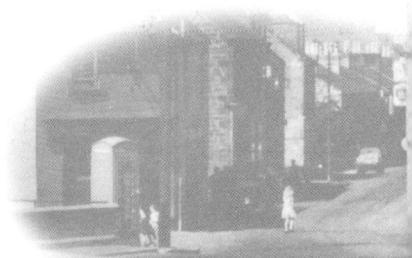

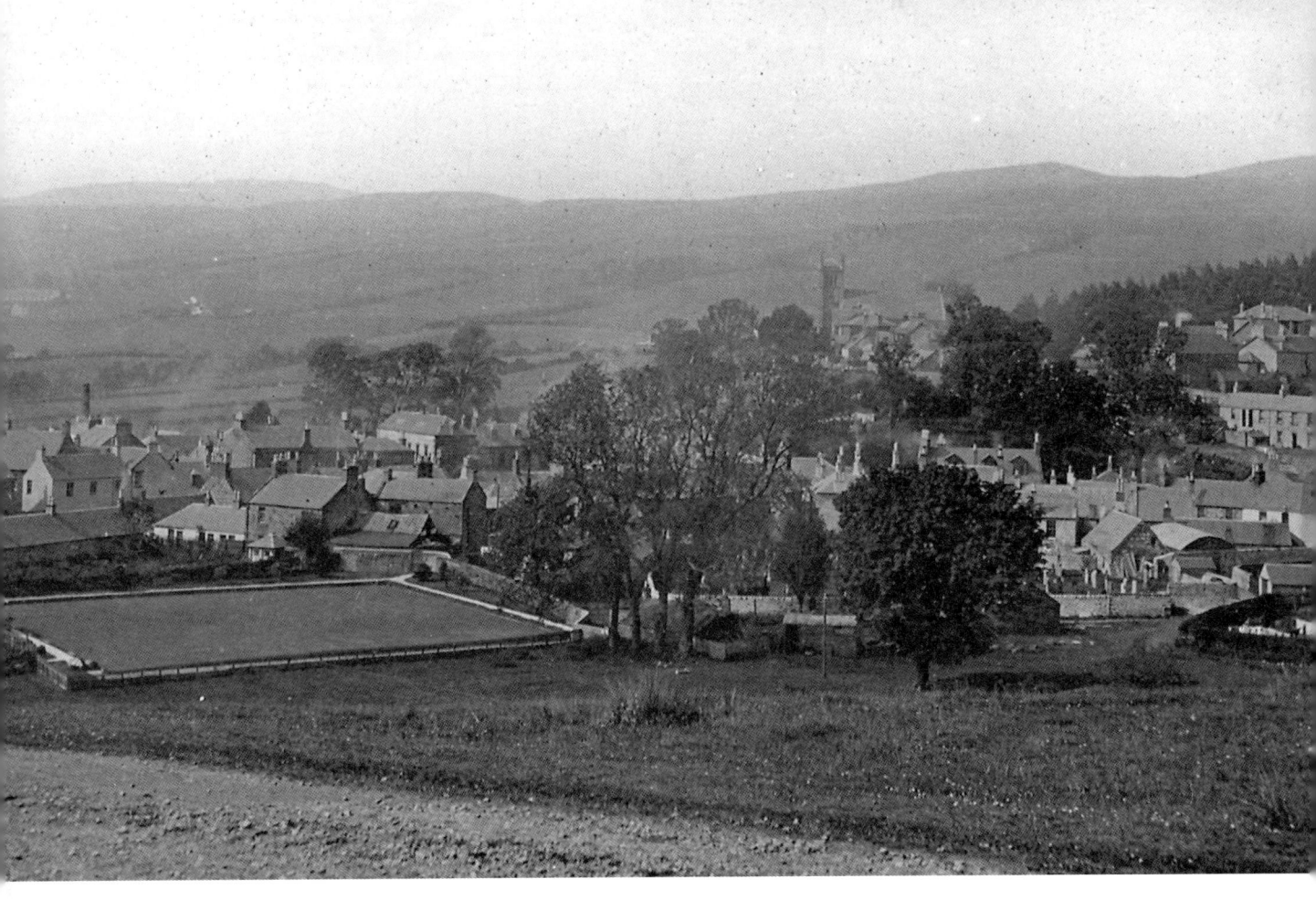

View from Cockie Knowe

The War Memorial is located on an elevated piece of ground known as Cockie Knowe. This view overlooks the bowling green, where Dalmellington Bowling Club play their games. The ground that the green is located on was at one time part of the Gaa Trust properties. Dalmellington Bowling Club, which was established in 1875, is the oldest bowling club in the valley.

Immediately behind the bowling green to the right are the buildings of New Street, known locally at one time as Crystal Palace Row. The long single storey row behind the bowling green is Cathcartson. In the distance, the tall round chimney stalk belongs to the gas works, which was located in Croft Street. This gas works were closed around 1926, the year that electricity was introduced to the village. The first gas works were opened in December 1842 by Robert Smith on his property at the back of the old Post Office in High Street. He installed a gasometer that was eight feet in diameter and six feet deep, which could contain 300 cubic feet of gas. The works were constructed by M. Shaw of Loanhead, near Edinburgh. When the works opened the post office and reading room were lit up, being a great novelty at the time. The works were within a few years relocated to larger premises at the top of Townhead.

In the centre of the picture can be seen the old kirkyard, and at its right-hand side is the smithy, around 1900 operated by T. Campbell Murray, blacksmith and jobber and by the First World War by Ivie Auld. This is identifiable by the Dutch barn-shaped building. The smithy building was the original manse of the parish, before the later manse was erected out the road to Pennyvenie. The field to the right of the bowling green was acquired for a playpark in 1936, and was named King George's Field in honour of the king.

On the right-hand side of the picture, the light-coloured buildings between the trees, are located in The Path, and at the turn of the century were mainly rented by miners.

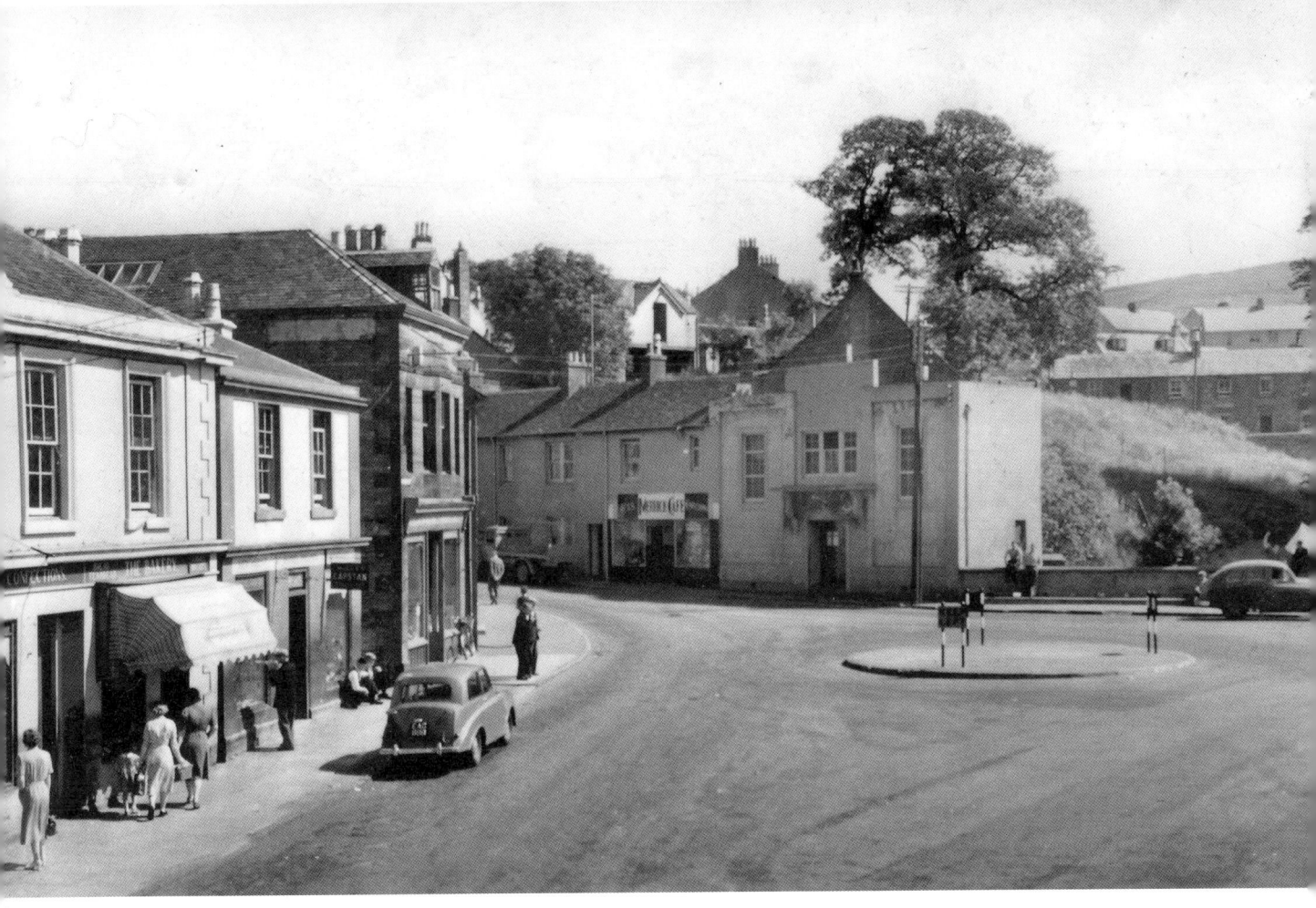

Square

Taken from an upstairs window in the butcher's shop at the end of Waterside Street, this picture shows the town centre. The shops on the left of the picture were occupied by MacCallum the baker, Bridgend Cafe (with the sun shade), and David Brown, newsagent, tobacconist and stationers. The taller building, after the narrow entry-way, was William Ritchie Stewart's grocery. It was taken over by Messrs Scott and Simpson, who continued as grocers.

At the foot of High Main Street can be seen the Merrick Café, run by the Bertellottis. In 1935 they advertised their fish suppers and invited customers to come and 'hear our new super radiogram'. The café was opened in the late 1920s, the building occupying the site of a row of single-storey buildings, formerly weavers' houses. These suffered in a major flood in the town in 1872 and again in 1927. The Muck Water, which takes a sharp turn behind them, failed to do so, and the waters burst through the house. Images exist of the water pouring through the windows onto the street.

To the right of the café is the Merrick Hall, built in 1927 as a billiard saloon, dance hall and meeting place. The proprietor was Mrs Bertellotti, followed by John Anderson, who made additions and alterations in 1940. The architect was Thomas McGill Cassels of Ayr. Many events took place in the building until it was closed in the 1960s. Amongst these was a soiree held in April 1945 to celebrate the return to the village of Corporal John Aitken RA and Sergeant Brown RA, both of Bellsbank Crescent, who had returned on leave from overseas. The Rev T. Nicholson presented the guests with money.

The Bertellottis came to Dalmellington from Kilmarnock, where they had immigrated to from Italy. A son, Armando (Andy), married a Scots girl, Kathy, in 1936 and settled in Dalmellington for a time. They were to emigrate to the United States in 1962. Anna Fiorina Hess, daughter of Andy and Kathy, wrote a fictional account of her family in a novel, *Born in Internment*, published in 2015. Next door to the Merrick Café was a surgery.

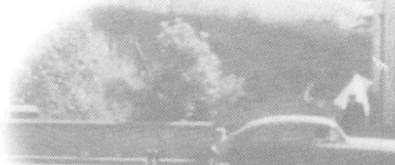

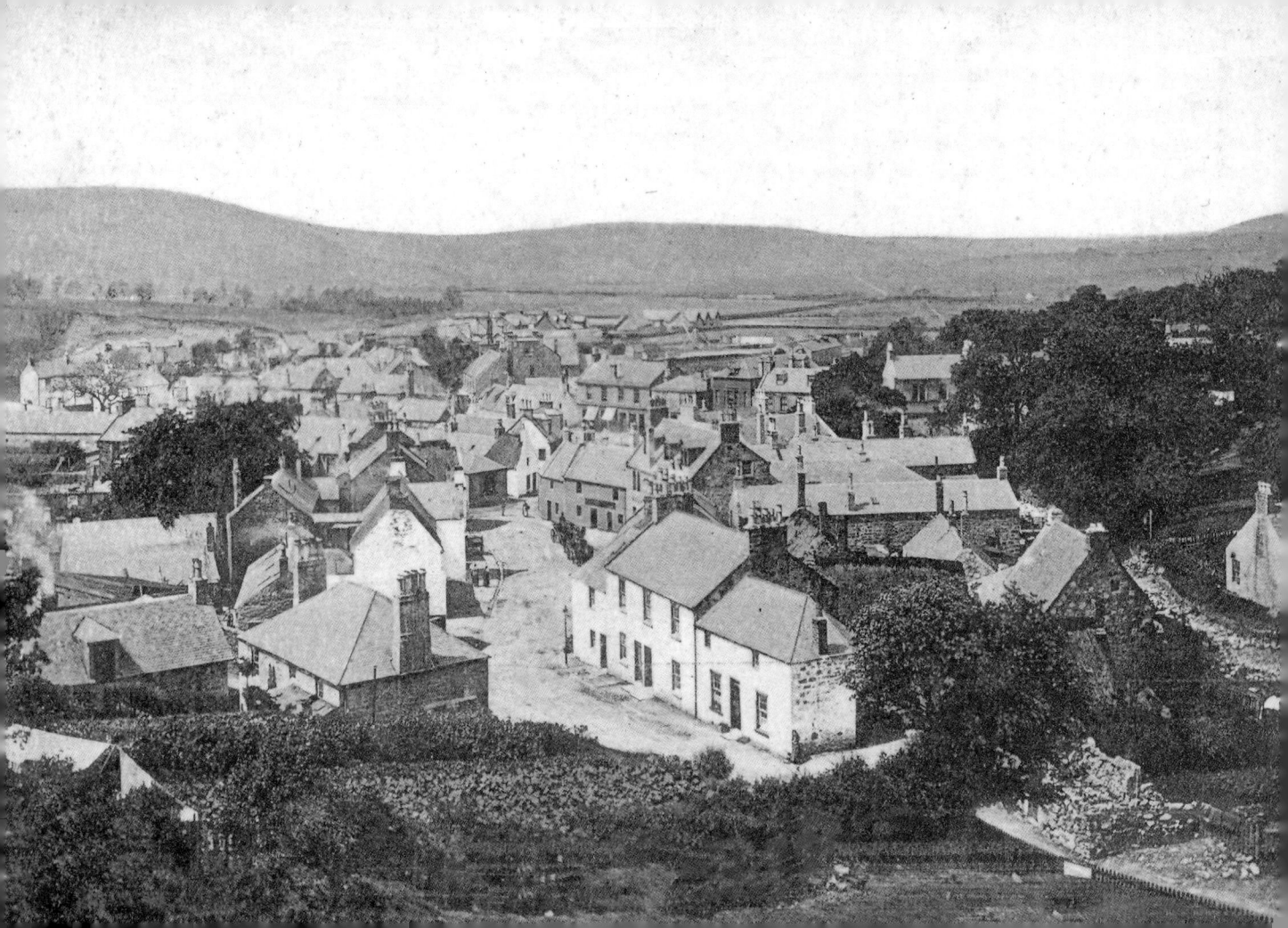

High Street from Motte

The elevated position of Dalmellington motte hill has been used to advantage to obtain this picture of the east end of the High Street. The picture was taken sometime after 1895 – the Black Bull Hotel being a good indicator of the date. The white-washed buildings in the foreground date from the nineteenth century, if not before. Soon after the ironworks were opened in 1847 a branch of the Edinburgh and Glasgow Bank was opened in the farthest part of this row, with the lamp post outside it. This bank fell into financial difficulties and was taken over by the Clydesdale Bank in 1858. The bank remained in the village until 1880, the last manager being John MacGeachin, the bank probably closing due to loss of trade to the Royal Bank. When this building was sold, the bank had a clause added to the title deeds preventing the building being passed on to any other bank.

Across the street is MacWhirter's bakery, the building with the hipped gable and tall chimney stalks. It lies at the foot of Townhead. Behind it is the gable end of the Cross Keys Inn. Behind it is Dr Jamieson's house. He was born here on 29 January 1789. After studying at Edinburgh University, he practised as a surgeon and apothecary in Alloa from 1819. In his spare time he built his own printing press, studied botany and wrote poems. Many of his works were published in the *Stirling Journal*. He died on 26 July 1826 when descending Ben Cleuch, in the Ochil Hills, plunging 200 feet into a ravine. He had apparently taken a short cut, intending to visit a patient in Tillicoultry. He left a widow, who died in Dunfermline.

Across the Muck Water can be seen the end of a row of cottages. At the end of this row were stepping stones across the water. In the bottom right of the picture can be seen the ruins of old cottages which were cleared away and the three cottages known as Trinidad were built on the site in 1910.

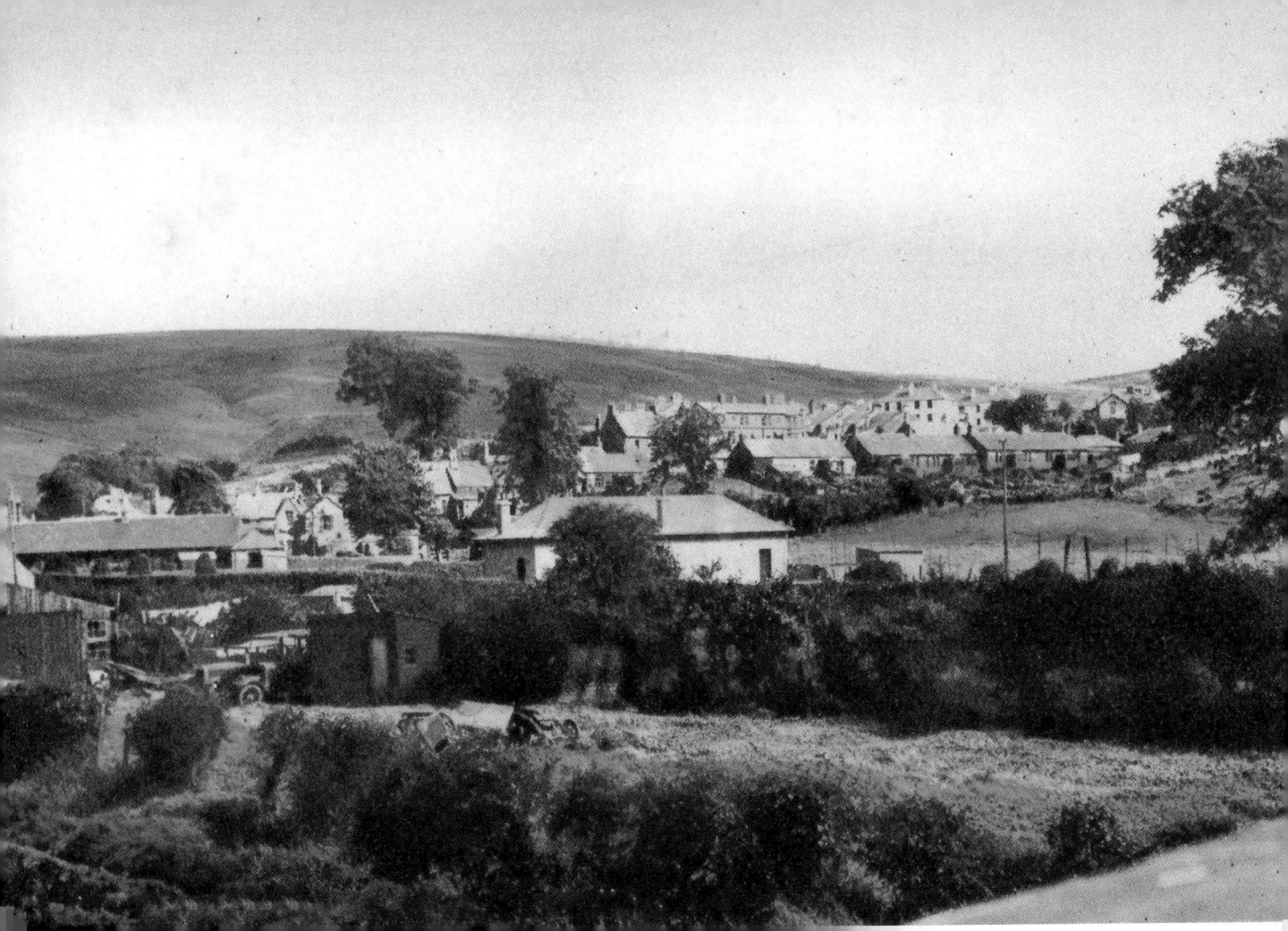

Townhead from MacClymont's Bridge

In the 1920s onwards there was a lot of new house building around the historic core of Dalmellington. This picture was taken from MacClymont's Bridge, looking due east towards Castlecrofts, where a number of new council houses were built off Castle Road in Castle Croft and Newbiggin Terrace. The picture predates the erection of the chapel.

The motte hill is seen to the left, next to an old tree. The rows of houses on either side of Townhead can be seen in front of it, the street better known locally as the Gas Brae. This was because the original gas works in the village was located at the top end of the street, but this was moved to a larger site in Croft Street. Townhead was the original main road heading south out of Dalmellington but it was originally very narrow, it still is, and rather steep, meaning that a New Road was built to the east, and Carsphairn Road to the south.

Almost all of the original weavers' cottages which were located in Townhead have been demolished, and replaced with later buildings, some of which are now quite old themselves. At the foot of the road was a building, sadly demolished known locally as the Laird's House, or the Schaw House. Tradition claims that it was built by one of the men responsible for taking part in the massacre of Glen Coe in 1692. What is certain, however, is that the building belonged to the Schaw family, who owned Keirs Castle and Grimmet estate. The building had a stone in the wall, bearing the Schaw arms, complete with the initials MIS and AIS, referring to Magister John Schaw and his wife. A John Schaw of Keirs also owned the lands of Camlarg at one time.

At the top of the street is an old cottage, known locally as the Drover's Cottage, which is said to date from 1724. Between the Drover's and Laird's houses the buildings in Townhead are of various dates, the most recent houses built being a terrace of eight homes, erected in 2005 on the site of St Barbara's Roman Catholic Church.

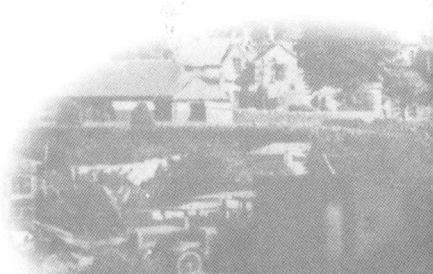

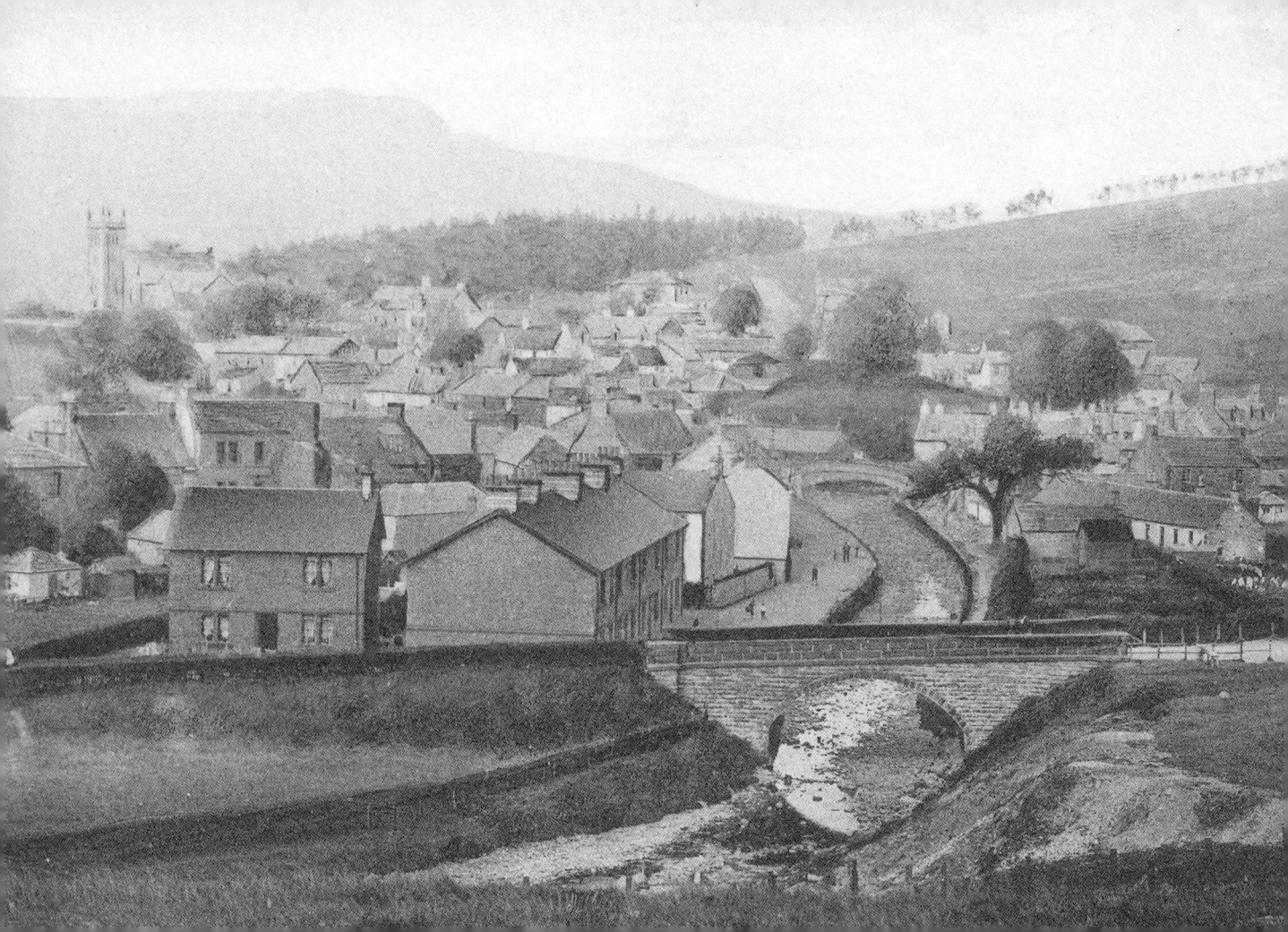

MacClymont's Bridge

Bellsbank and Carsphairn roads form an early by-pass around Dalmellington, created some time around 1803, when Quintin MacAdam of Berbeth (now Craigengillan) laid out a new route to ease traffic flow between Ayr and Castle Douglas. MacAdam was also a member of the Ayrshire Turnpike Trustees, and as such had a considerable interest in promoting road improvements. He was appointed as chairman of the Ayr to Dalmellington committee in 1795. The route of the new Dalmellington by-pass may have been planned out by Bryce MacQuiston, who produced a plan of the roadway. The road apparently cost £400 to make, paid for by MacAdam, and took four years to construct, requiring to pass over what was mossy and unstable ground. MacClymont's Bridge was constructed as part of this roadway, crossing the Muck Water. It has never been satisfactorily explained who the MacClymont, after whom the bridge was named, was.

In this picture, the double-storey house facing Bellsbank Road was erected in 1903 by Dalmellington Iron Company, as was the tenement block facing Waterside Street. In 1914, of the 22 houses, 19 were occupied by colliers, the other three by a labourer, an oversman and a fireman. The building behind the tenements, with its gable facing the burn, was at one time Dalmellington's school. It served as such from the 1830s until 1875, when the new school board building was opened.

The building to the left of the picture, with the hipped roof, is currently known as Dalmellington House. The building is now owned by the Princess Royal Trust East Ayrshire Carers, and since 2009 has been run as a guesthouse, with some funding from East Ayrshire Council and NHS Ayrshire and Arran. The house dates from the 1860s, having been built on the site of older thatched cottages.

Dalmellington House was originally known as Hollybank House and for many years was the home of the village doctor. At one time it was home to Dr Robert MacLachlan, who served in the village for twenty years, dying in 1895. He was followed by Dr Robert Dunlop and Dr Ee Seng Lee.

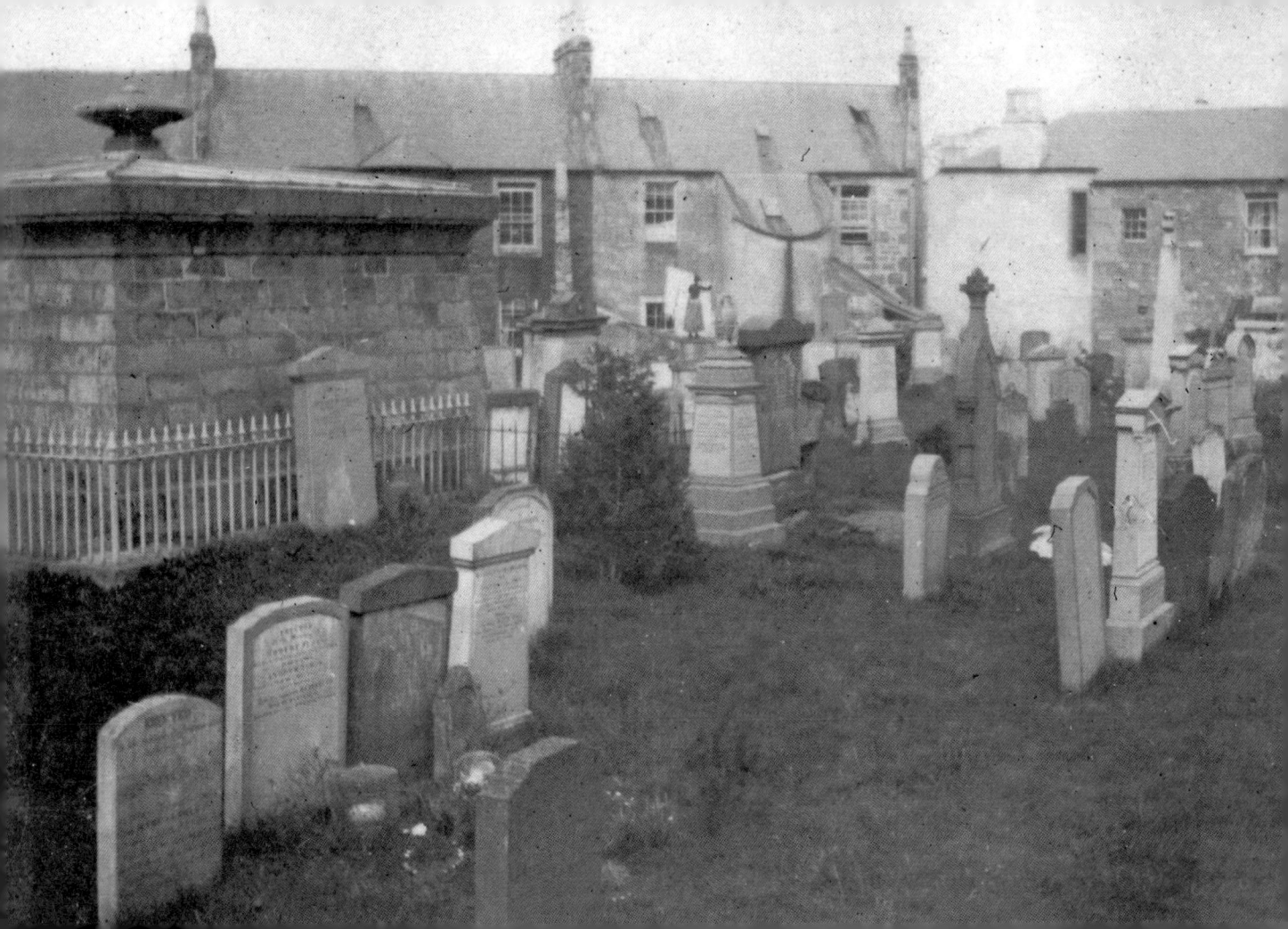

Old Kirkyard

The old kirkyard in the centre of Dalmellington is where the parish church once stood. When a church was first established here cannot now be determined, but this was where it remained until 1766, when the present church hall was erected as the new church. The old church building was thereafter used as a school up until the 1830s, after which it was demolished.

The parish of Dalmellington was established in the twelfth or thirteenth century, indicating that a church would have been created. In 1501 the church was annexed to the Chapel Royal of Stirling. This old photograph shows the number of stones that formerly existed within the burial ground. The photographer is looking north-west, towards the gap through to the High Street. To the left is the back of the houses of New Street, with a woman hanging her washing on the line.

The light-coloured building in the centre is the back of Ye Old Castle House. The large structure to the left, surrounded by railings, is the MacAdam of Craigengillan mausoleum. This was erected in the 1860s as the burial place of the local landowners, even although Craigengillan is actually in the parish of Straiton.

Also in the kirkyard is a granite memorial commemorating all of the Covenanters of the parish, although it does not mention them by name. It was erected in 1929. When the Solemn League and Covenant was being signed, 222 parishioners subscribed, but 179 of these were unable to write their names. Colonel Thomas Buchan had a garrison in the village, home to soldiers who searched for the Covenanters, and in 1678 the 'Highland Host' of 900 rough soldiers was quartered here. Covenanters from Dalmellington include John Paterson of Pennyvenie, Quintin Dick, and Roger Dun of Benquhat. Paterson and Dick survived, though not without spells of torture, imprisonment and living rough. Dick lived in the village, was imprisoned in 1684 and was due to be banished the following year, but was left for dead. He survived a number of years. Dun was killed following Carsphairn Fair and is buried in that village.

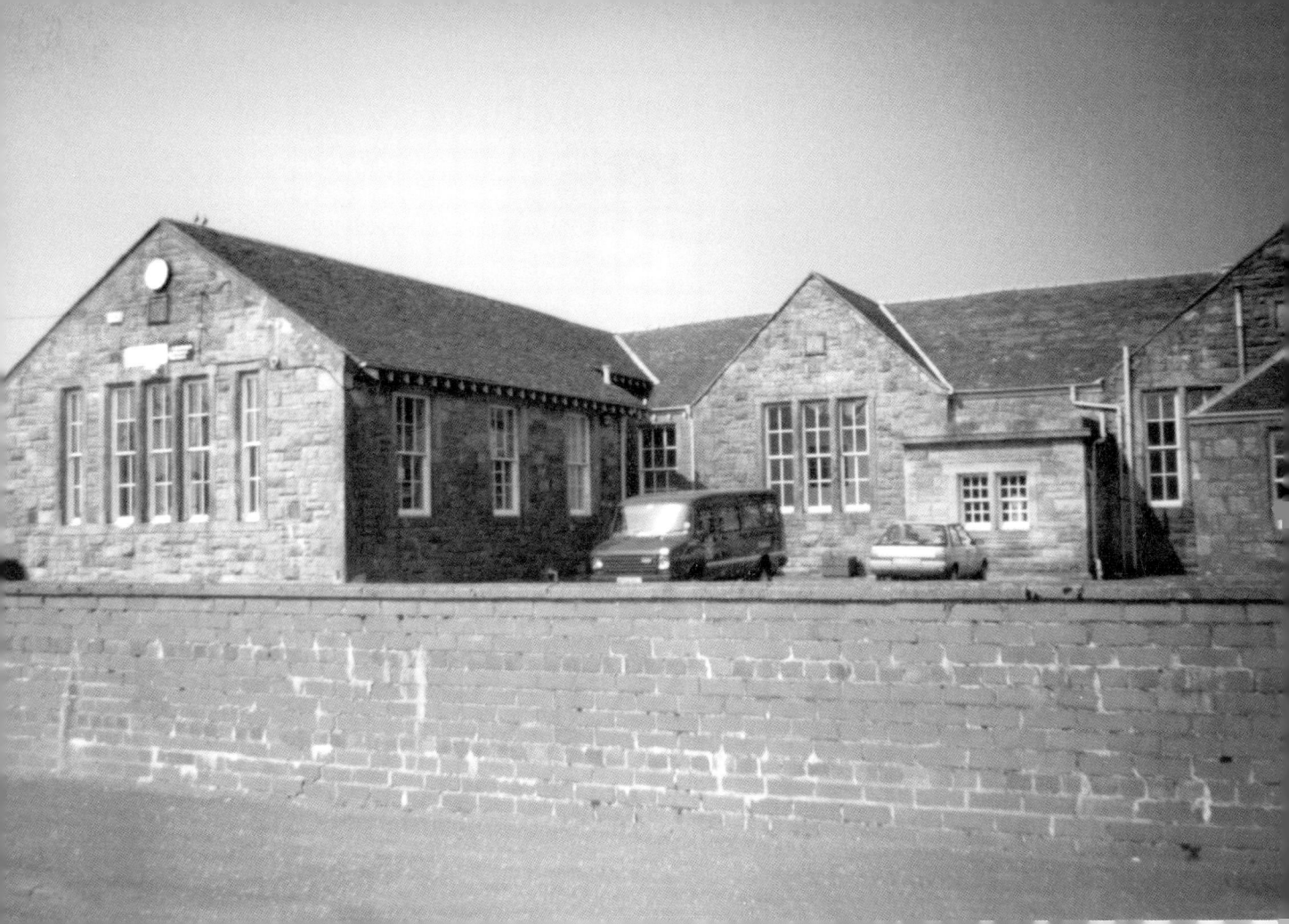

Dalmellington School

The oldest school in Dalmellington was probably established soon after the Reformation of 1560 and may have been held in the church itself. Some of the earliest known schoolmasters are from the seventeenth century – James Stuart was in charge in 1691 before he left to train for the ministry. The next dominie was probably William Cargill.

In 1766 the school moved into part of the old church in the kirkyard, where it remained until 1818. In 1850 the school moved to a building erected in Waterside Street, where it remained until 1876.

In 1874 the new Dalmellington Public School was erected in Ayr Road, shown here. The ground for it was gifted by Charlotte MacAdam Cathcart in 1873. Adjoining it was a schoolmaster's house. The school and house were designed by Brown and Lawrence and was erected at a cost of £3,000. A 'temporary' building was erected in 1919 as a junior secondary school. A new brick-built building was added in 1930 to house the infant school, designed by William Reid, county architect. By 1951 Dalmellington Junior Secondary School had 550 primary pupils plus over 200 secondary pupils. Pupils aged over fifteen could travel to Ayr Academy to continue their studies if they wished.

In 1973-78 a large new Doon High School was erected, complete with an indoor swimming pool, designed by Ayr County Council architects. The building cost in excess of £500,000. The first pupils moved in at the start of session 1975-76. Work on the school was still incomplete, and it wasn't until March 1978 that the building was officially opened by regional councillor, Willie Goudie. The former school shown here became Dalmellington Primary School, and as such it continued until 1998, when the school was closed and the pupils moved into part of the Doon Academy building. The building was subsequently used by the Book Town then demolished. The roll at Doon Academy in 1992 was 328. By 2016 the roll had fallen to 318, and Dalmellington Primary School had 110 pupils.

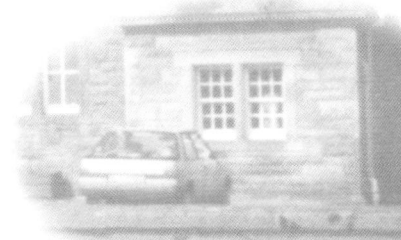

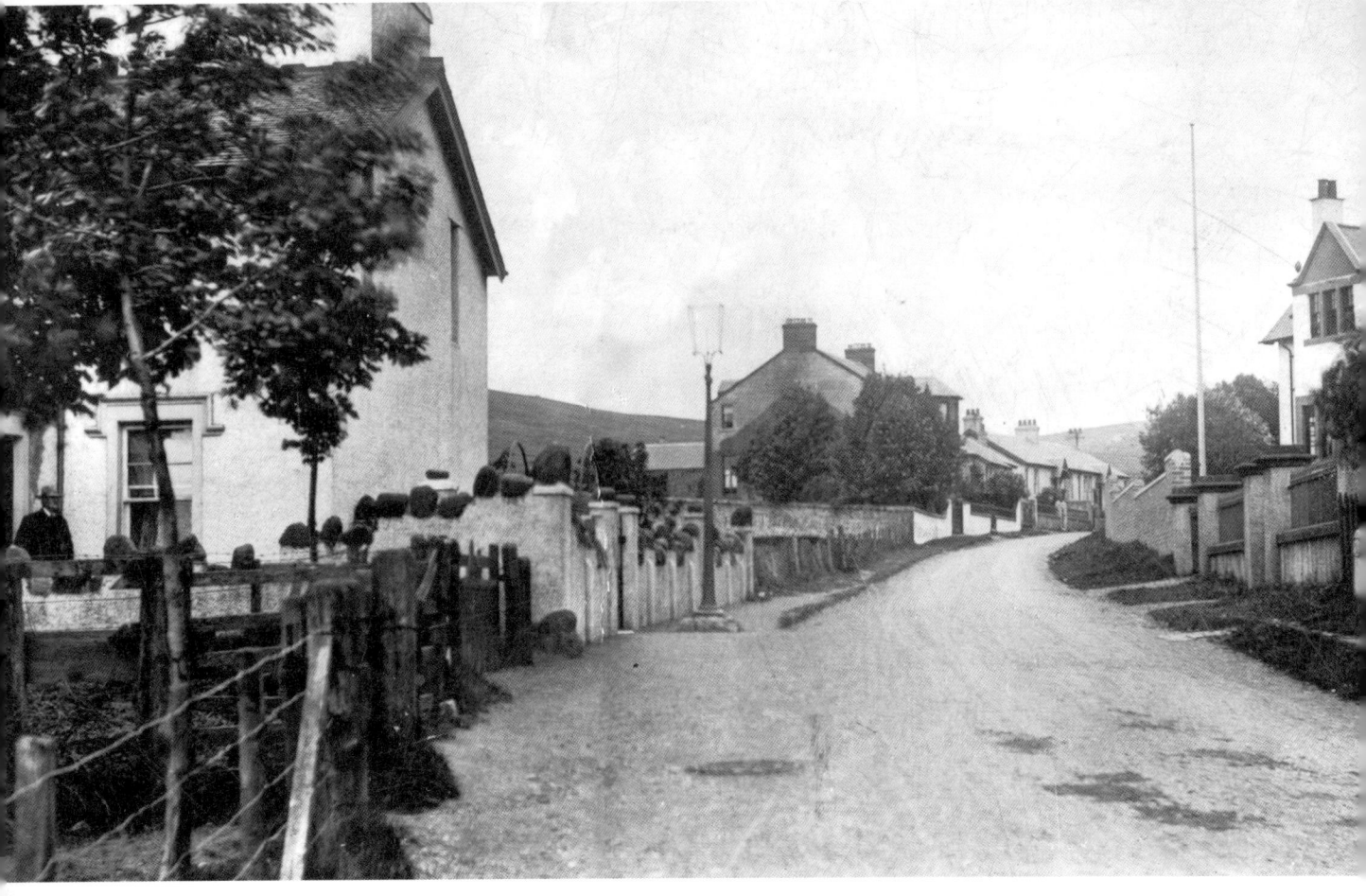

Meadowbank

Carsphairn Road leads out of the village heading south. The first buildings to be erected here was a row of eleven houses known as Meadowbank. These were built in the last few decades of the nineteenth century, probably by Hugh Gibson, builder, who owned them. In the early twentieth century, a number of larger villas were built in this part of the village, including one belonging to Walter Bain, a shipping agent, whose office was in Barns Street, Ayr. He was a part-owner of the Ayr Steam Shipping Company, which operated in the latter half of the nineteenth century, with a fleet of steamers, plying between Glasgow, Ayr and some Irish ports. He was also a director with the Laird Line. Bain also served as a county councillor, representing Dalmellington. He latterly lived at Derclach, a large villa in Ayr. Craiglee, located in what was known as Back Road, was owned by John Clark, draper, whose shop was in Main Street. John Clark died in 1911 aged 52 and is buried in the cemetery.

The large house on the left of the picture is known as Ladywell. This was the home of Hugh Gibson, owner of the Meadowbank houses. He also owned a number of other properties in the village, in particular in Townhead, New Street and High Street. The large house on the right-hand side of the road is known as Rathan, erected around 1905 in the Arts and Craft style. This was the home of John Blair Cook, English master at Dalmellington High School at the start of the twentieth century. He served as a Lieutenant Colonel in the Royal Scots Fusiliers during the First World War and was awarded the Distinguished Service Order, Military Cross and the French Croix de Guerre. However, he was killed on 24 November 1917 aged 36 and is buried in the Jerusalem War Cemetery.

Around 1950 a house in Carsphairn Road was purchased by the Parish Church to serve as the new manse, the old manse at the Glebe being too large for church purposes and in need of major repairs.

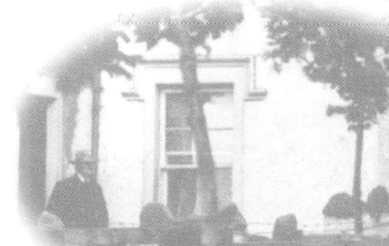

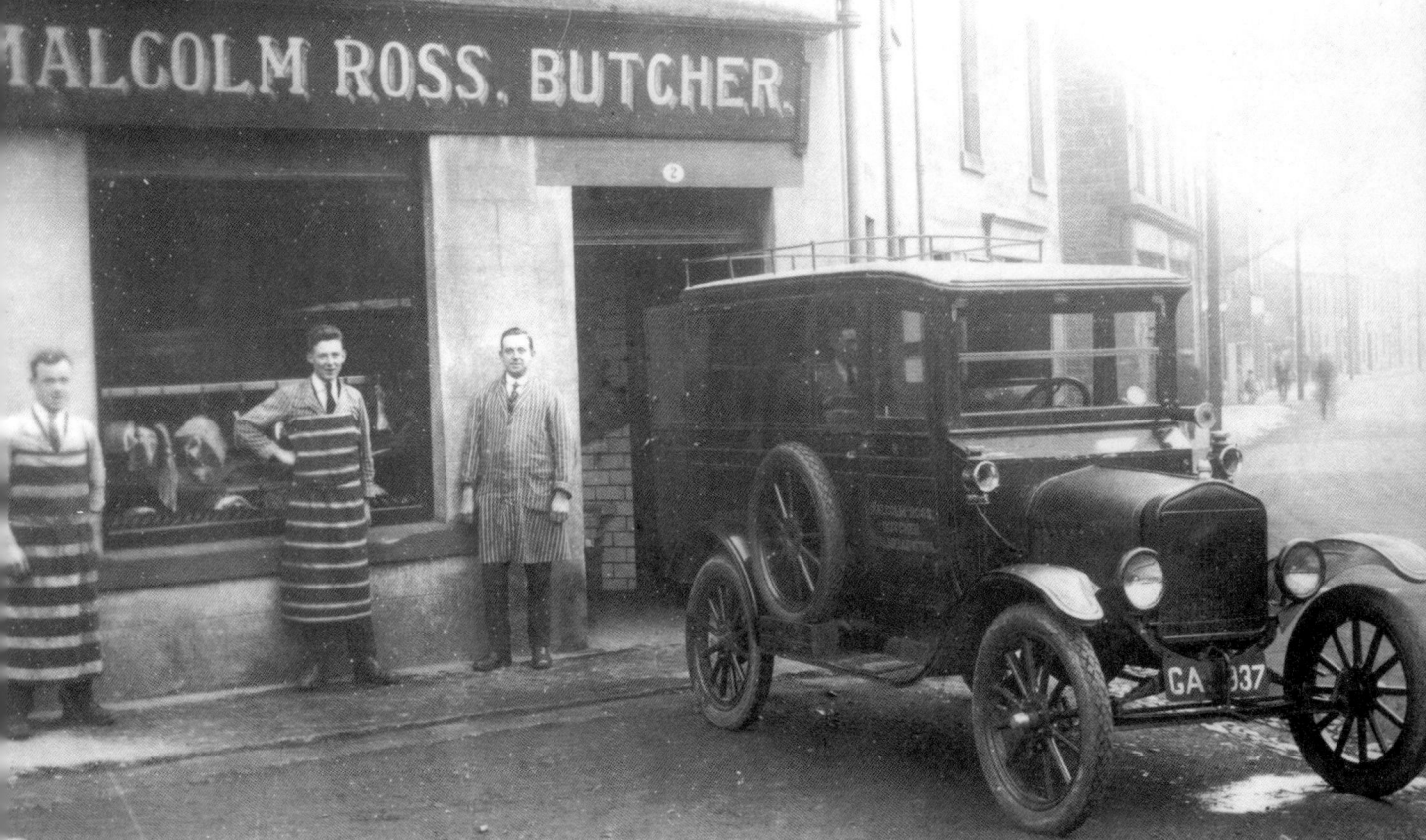

Malcolm Ross's Butchers

At one time there were buildings joined on to the frontage of this shop, extending into the street, terminating in line with Croft Street. They were weavers' houses, but they appear to have been demolished around 1900, giving easier access to Waterside Street and allowing Low Main Street to be widened, making the corner more suitable for passing traffic. Soon after the buildings had been removed, the shop was rebuilt as a butchery.

The first business to occupy the new premises was owned by Thomas MacFarlane, a flesher, who ran the Central Meat Market from here. MacFarlane was succeeded in the business by John Murray, who ran the shop around the time of the First World War. The butchery was taken over by Malcolm Ross, sometime after the Great War. At the start of the twentieth century William Ross was a flesher, or butcher, with premises in High Main Street. Malcolm Ross is seen in this picture standing to the right, nearest the door. Ross was one of three early shop-keepers who put delivery vans on the road, around 1935. The others were R. & J. Templeton Ltd, and Brown & MacCallum, bakers. The van seen in this picture, an old Morris, was used to deliver butcher meat to various local mining communities, such as Pennyvenie, Benquhat and Waterside. Malcolm Ross was succeeded in the business by J. & M. Paterson, James Paterson being followed by William Paterson.

There were other butcher shops in the village. One of these was run by James Burns, located in the High Street at the time of the First World War. Another butcher was George Orr & Sons, who operated a butcher's shop and grocery in the High Street in the 1960s.

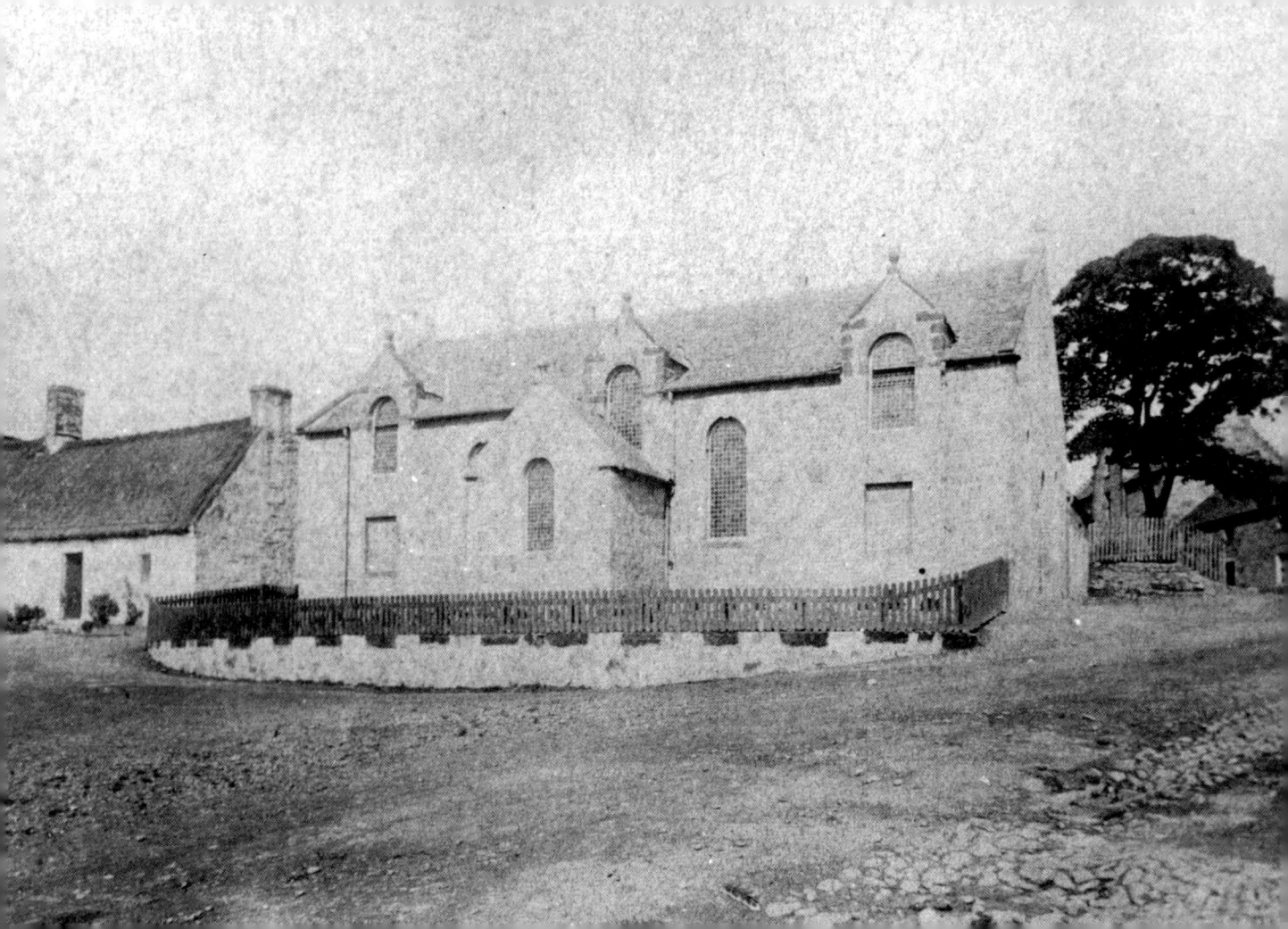

Dalmellington Old Church

This is an early picture of Dalmellington Parish Church as it was before the building was rebuilt as a church hall. The church was originally erected in 1766, during the ministry of Rev Duncan MacMyne. He was the son of the local schoolmaster and following his training to be a minister was ordained on 15 September 1762. He remained at Dalmellington until he died in 1799 at the age of sixty. He never married. The church was erected at a spot then known as Kiln-knowe-fold, indicating that an old lime-kiln may have been located nearby. The church cost £240 to build and measured 50 feet by 24 feet internally, large enough for 442 worshippers. Lofts were positioned to either end, and at a later date the North, or Laird's Aisle was added for the MacAdams of Berbeth. When the church was opened, it had a new pulpit, precentor's desk, baptismal font and a seat for the minister. The rest of the church seating was either transferred from the old kirk in the graveyard, or else supplied by those who had a right to them.

Following a number of years used as a lodging house and hall, in March 1883 Rev George Hendrie wrote to the Hon. Col Augustus Cathcart asking if the parish church could have the building as a church hall. No reply was received until Spring 1887 when a letter arrived asking for the names and designations of the kirk session, so that their names may be included in the Deed of Gift. The church became owners in 1887, but it was not until 18 April 1888 that the new church hall was officially opened. In the intervening period, the building had to be restored, at a cost of £400. Of this, £210 was raised in two months. The memorial stone was laid with masonic honours by the local master of the lodge, John Wilson, who was also a church elder. The event was preceded by a march through the village, led by Dalmellington Band, which included the church organisations, in addition to the Free Gardeners, Loyal Orange Lodge and Good Templars.

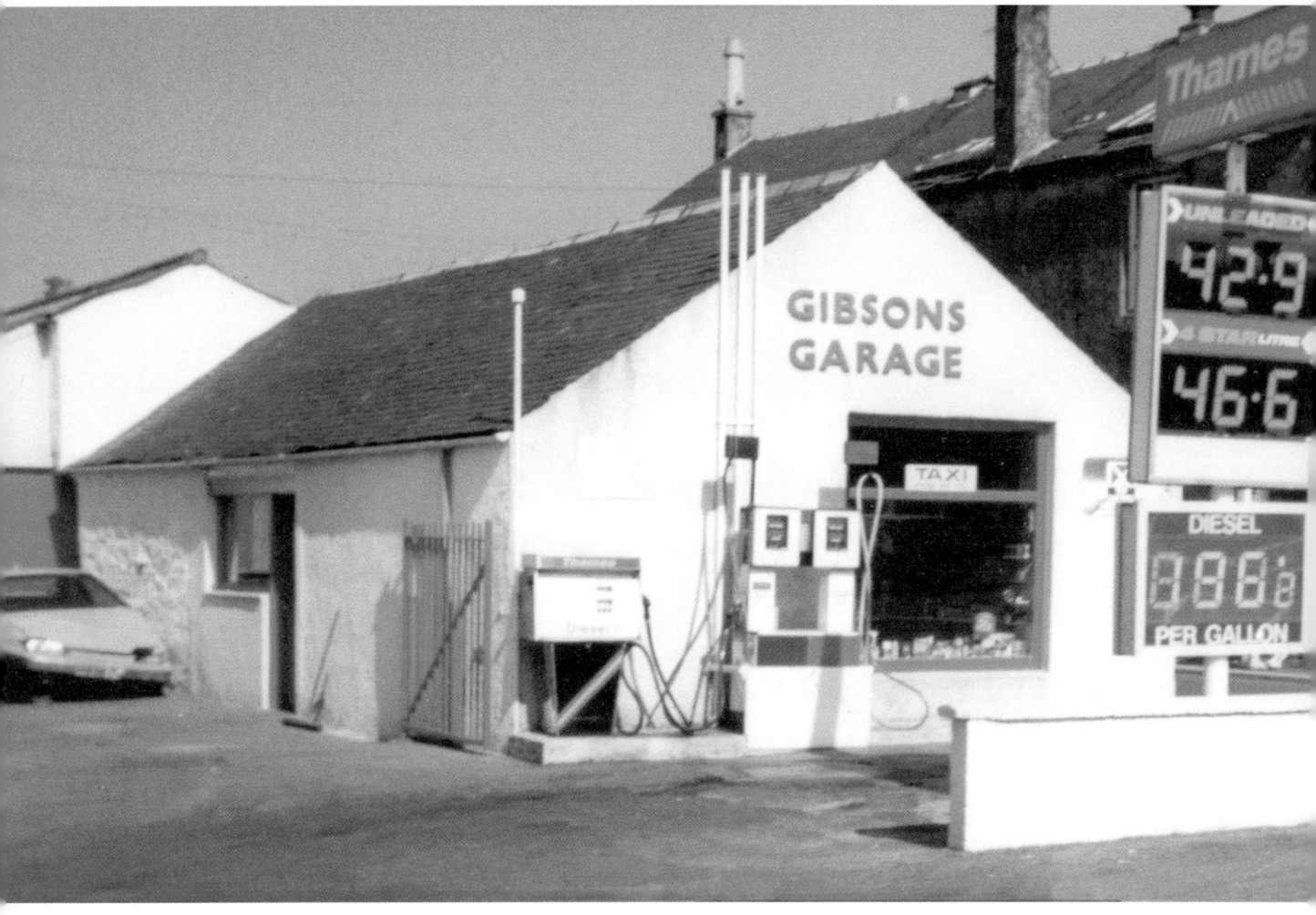

Gibson's Garage

The Gibson family have been prominent businessmen in the village for many years. The garage shown here was built on the site of three old weavers' cottages which were demolished. At the start of the First World War they were owned by Alexander Gibson, game dealer, who lived in one of them. James Gibson lived at the turn of the twentieth century, and he was one of the first people in the village to have a motor car. This was described as a very fine car, 'a sort of cross between a lorry and the then popular horse-drawn "brake"'. The garage was in existence from at least 1921. The garage was taken over by James's son, Alexander, better known to the locals as 'Sanny'. The next person to run the garage was Sanny's son, James Gibson. When this photograph was taken, the garage sold Thames petrol and diesel. The price of the four star petrol, 46.6p per litre, indicates that the photograph dates from around 1990. The garage is now closed and part of the premises is occupied by the Rainbow sweet shop and gift shop.

At one time, there were other garages in Dalmellington, supplying the needs of the motorist. These included Napier's Garage, located in High Main Street, hiring motor cars and selling BP fuels, and Gemmell's Garage in Low Main Street, originally the stables and garage associated with the Eglinton Hotel. In Croft Street was Cullen's Garage, in addition to Croft Street Garage, the latter operated by John Ireland & Sons. The Ayr Road Garage was operated by John T. Maguire and Sons then David Murdoch. Tam Maguire was well-known in the area, operating the garage at Burnside and opening the Ayr Road Garage in 1957. He also ran a taxi service and died in 1967.

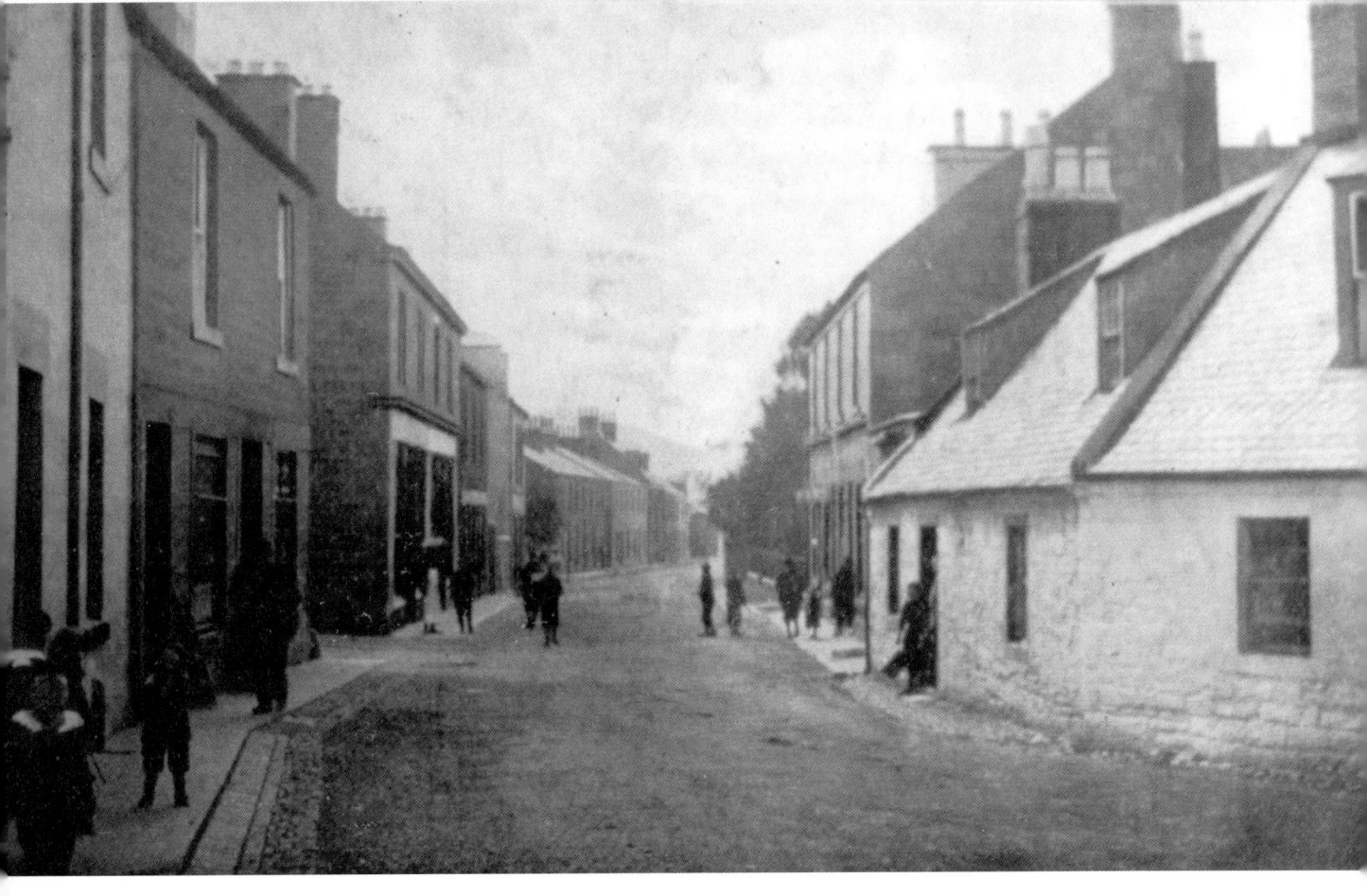

Main Street

This is an early photograph of the Main Street, looking west towards the Eglinton Hotel. There used to be a line of old cottages along the street in the early nineteenth century, but the arrival of the railway resulted in many of them being rebuilt or extended into commercial premises. For example, when the Royal Bank was erected, a number of single-storey thatched dwellings were removed. On the immediate left is Paterson's butcher's shop. The building next door had a shop on the ground floor, occupied in the first half of the twentieth century by John Clark & Son, draper and milliner. It was later occupied by W. & M. Johnstone as a newsagent and stationery shop and then Costcutters. Across the lane, the shop with the white sign was James Napier's newsagent.

Other former businesses which operated in Main Street include Neil Bell & Son, baker; John MacDowall, draper and outfitters; John Bain & Sons, drapers; J. & J. Dalziel, fruiterer and florist; George Cron, merchant and ironmonger; William Smith, ladies' and gents' tailors, and James MacCulloch, draper and clothier. John MacCulloch established a bakery in 1852 and this was still operating in Low Main Street at the start of the twentieth century. Other bakers who operated from Main Street included Farquhar Scott. There were watchmakers and jewellers here too – Thomas L. Wright, John Graham and Thomas W. Wyllie, all in business at the start of the twentieth century.

The small white cottage on the right was one of the older buildings in Main Street. The left hand one had its front wall removed and moved back into line with the shops beyond; a second storey being added at the same time. The one on the right was totally demolished to allow the creation of Gibson's garage.

In more recent years, Low Main Street is where a factory was opened in 1967 by Jersey Kapwood, manufacturing lingerie. The factory was later acquired by East Ayrshire Council and rebuilt to form a one-stop shop, containing a medical centre, council office and dentist. This was opened on 25 June 2001.

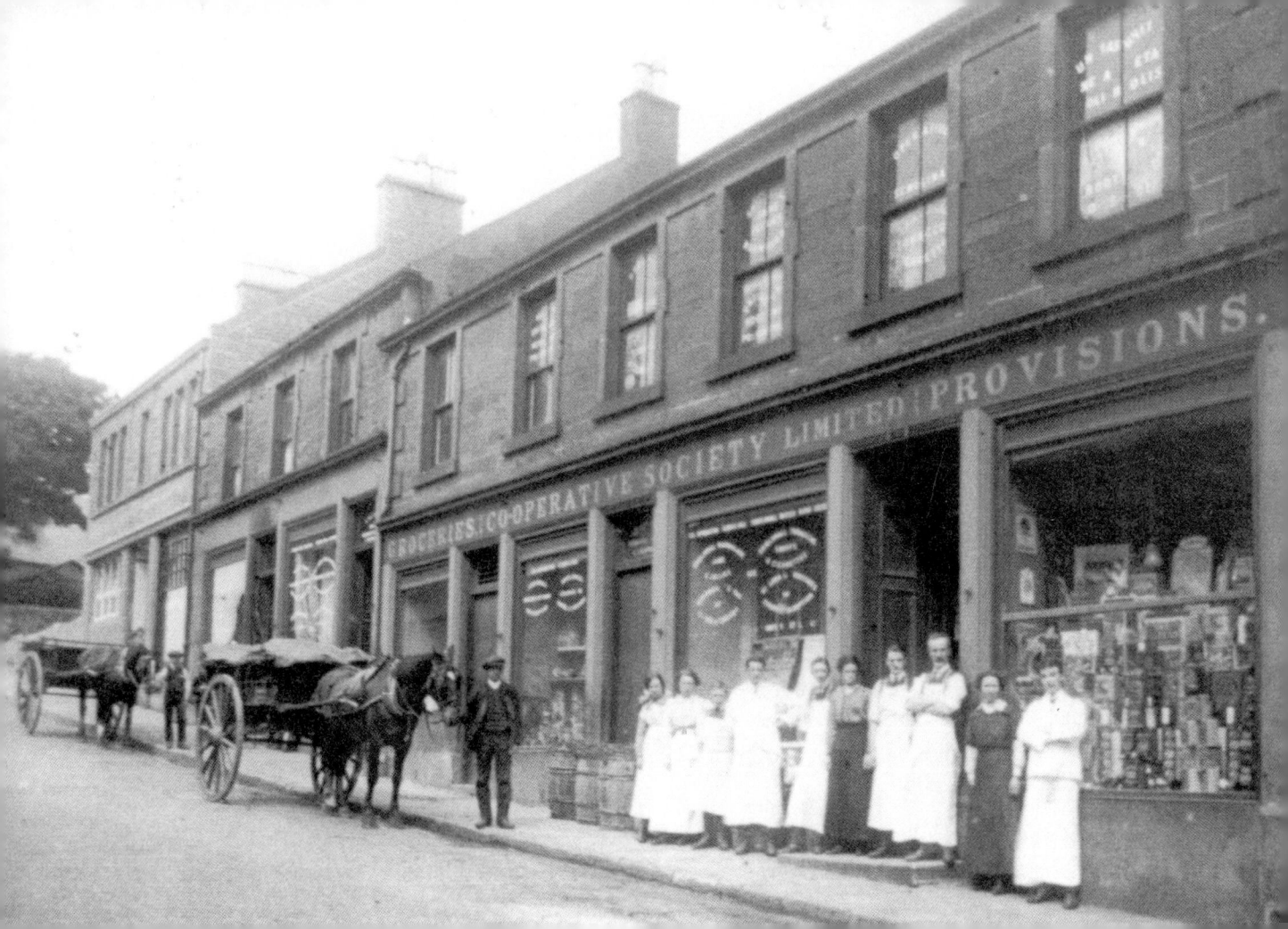

Dalmellington Co-operative

Dalmellington Co-operative Society was established in 1879, perhaps following a meeting in a house where the Merrick Hall was later to be built. One of the first shops was in High Main Street, next to the Gaa Institute, but this was later to become Fyfe's chemist shop (rebuilt for him in the 1930s). In 1882 the society joined the Central Co-operative Board, allowing it to benefit from greater buying power.

The society built commercial premises on the north side of High Main Street, shown here. The building to the right comprised three shop premises, two of which sold groceries and provisions. The first building was erected in 1883 to contain the grocery, bakery and drapery departments. However, within a few years this was found to be too small, and in 1896 a new building was added to the side at a cost of £474. The foundation stone was laid with masonic honours by the members of Dalmellington's Lodge St Thomas, one of only two such services they carried out – the other being at the renovation of the old church. It had a frontage of over thirty feet, divided into a bakery and drapery shop. On the first floor was a hall for general meetings plus a meeting room for the committee and an office for the secretary. In the group of buildings here there was also a granary, store, office and stables for the horses that pulled the co-operative's delivery carts.

In 1896, the society brought in sales of over £10,000, there being 280 members. A dividend payable to members was two shillings and nine pence, non-members receiving one shilling fourpence ha'penny.

The building at the end of the row was the post office for many years, perhaps its fourth location in the village. In 2017 the post office was closed and the agency for it was relocated to The Zone, a community facility located lower down High Main Street. The Zone Initiative was established in 2010 to provide facilities for children in the village.

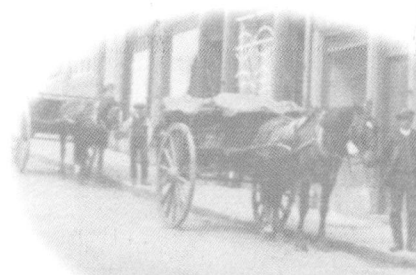

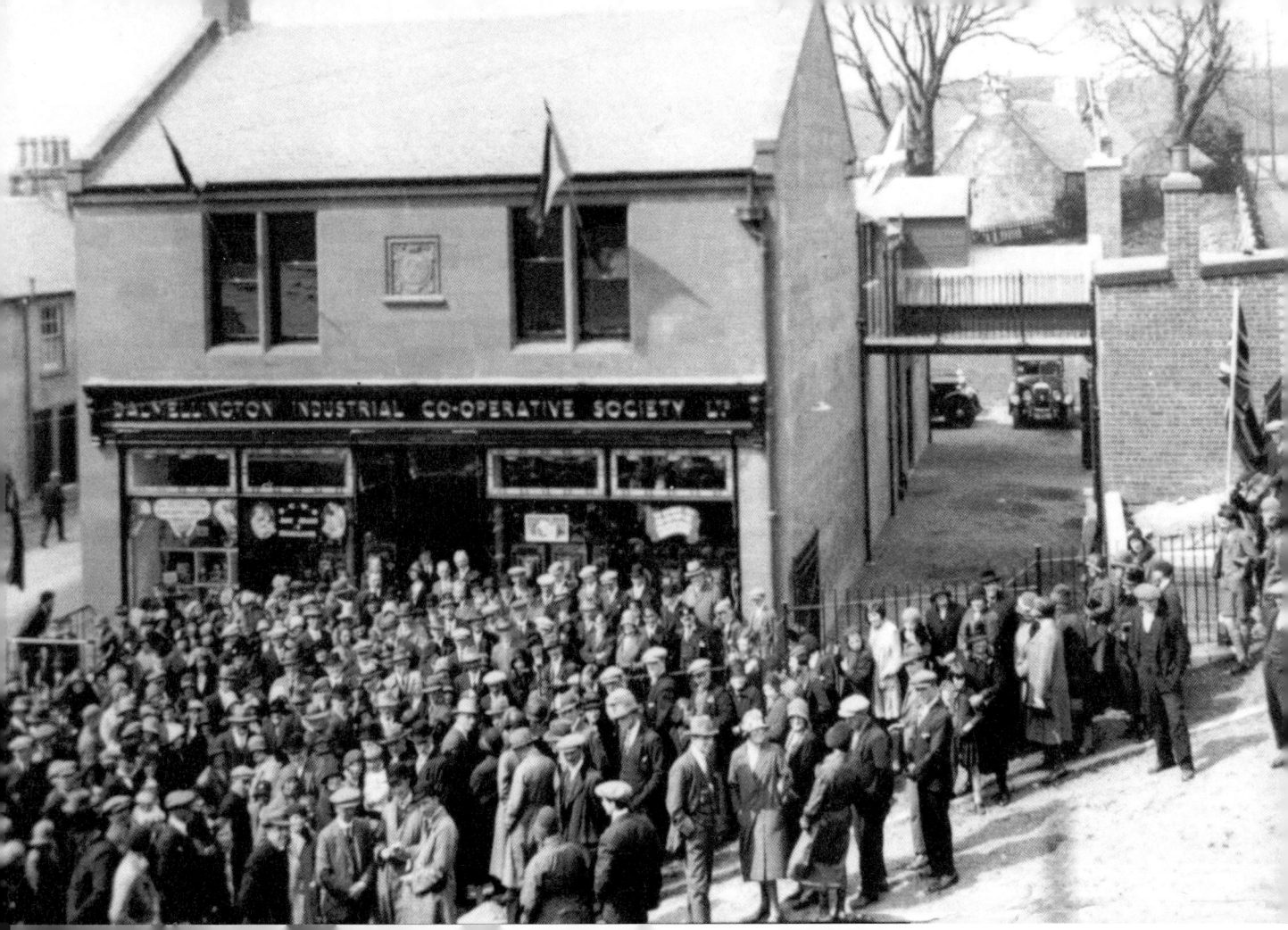

New Co-operative Shop

In 1931 a new co-operative store was opened in Church Hill, just at the junction of High Main Street. The picture shows the number of folk who attended the official opening. Children who were present were given a white handkerchief on which a representation of the new building was printed. The building was erected by Joseph Hyslop using Ballochmyle sandstone, and a carved stone with the co-op's logo was incorporated on the front façade, at first floor level.

The society was to purchase its first motorised van in 1958, allowing it to extend deliveries as far south as Dalry and to the mining villages in the valley. An Albion van, the customer entered by a door at the back, passed along a corridor and exited by a side door. It was self-service. The last manager of Dalmellington co-op was Alexander Sadler.

By 1951 the society employed 71 people and had a membership of 1,455. Of the employees, 48 worked in the shops and the delivery vans that visited local communities. A further ten worked in the bakery and other production facilities, seven did miscellaneous work and there were five managers. Turnover that year was £144,000, the dividend payable being 2 shillings and sixpence. The co-operative society was to merge with the Patna Co-operative Society before the national co-operative society took over. It continues to run the premises shown here as a general store. At one time the shop was known as Churchill (sic) Co-operative, but it has reverted to the Co-op foodstore name.

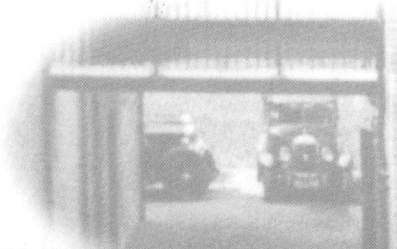

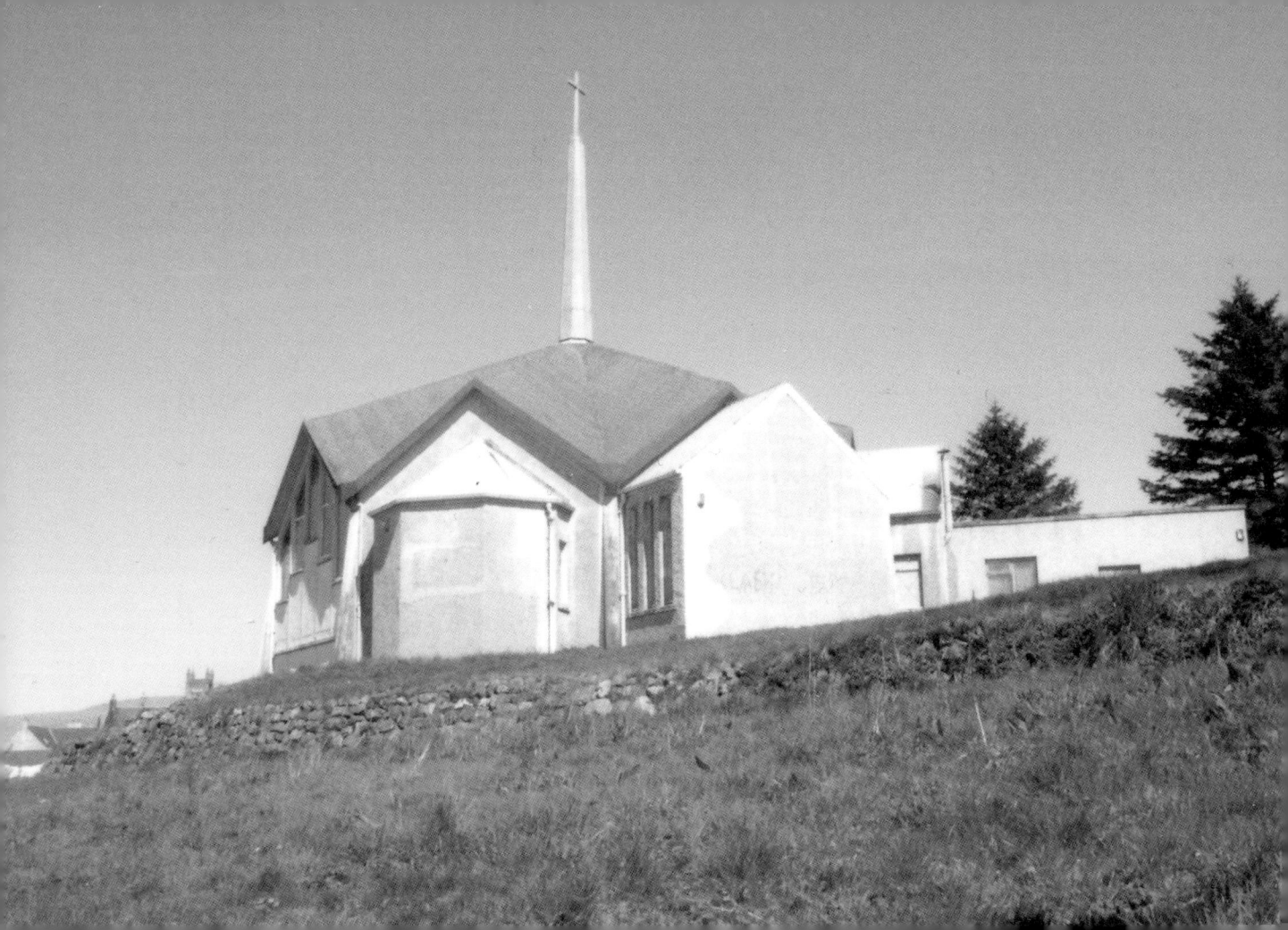

Our Lady & St Barbara's Church

The arrival of many Irish to the parish, to find work at the ironworks or in mining, meant that there was a need for a Roman Catholic place of worship. The first chapel was erected in Dalmellington in 1860, known as Our Lady of the Rosary. In 1895 a new chapel, hall, school and presbytery was erected at Waterside to serve the local Roman Catholics, known as St Francis Xavier's. At the time the church in Dalmellington was closed, though the building was retained as a church hall. The congregation at Waterside was to outgrow the chapel, and plans for a new chapel in Dalmellington were pursued, and at length Our Lady and St Barbara's Church was erected at Townhead on a site where old cottages had been cleared away. Rev John J. Quinn, the local priest, was instrumental in pushing for the new chapel.

An octagonal design was chosen, with slender spire, capable of holding 250 worshippers. The Roman Catholic church nationally was keen on modern church designs, and this was no exception. Erected from 1959-61, the cost of construction was £17,000. The architect was Charles W. Gray of Edinburgh, who designed a number of other chapels. The official opening took place on 9 April 1961, the Bishop of Galloway, Rt Rev Dr Joseph McGee performing the ceremony. The chapel was called Our Lady and St Barbara's, the latter name being the patron saint of miners. The mining connection was emphasised by a Davy Safety Lamp hanging from a coal pick in the sacristy. Father Quinn left the priesthood in 1962 and he was replaced by Rev Sean Murphy (1962-70), John Kane (1970-77), John Harkin (1977-80), John Kerr (1980-81), Alistair Tosh (1981-85) and Edward McGhee (1985-88).

With a falling attendance, the chapel was closed and the congregation was merged with Waterside once more, which was to serve all of the communities in the Doon valley. The chapel was put on the market in 1997 but with no purchasers it was demolished on 12 July 2003. The site was later built on, with houses facing onto Townhead, much as the old cottages had done fifty years earlier.

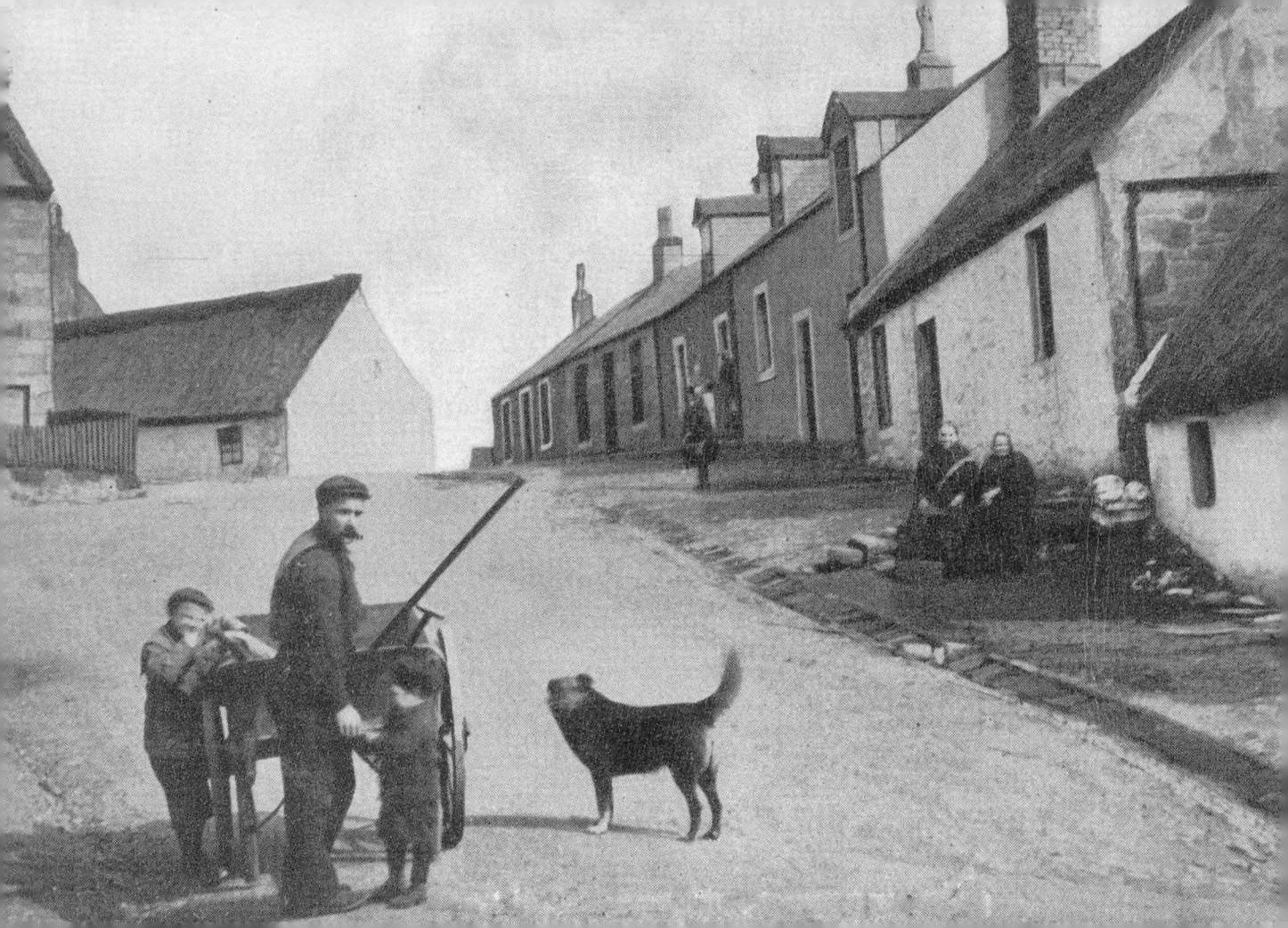

Church Hill

This old postcard view (published by M. & M. Gemmell of Dalmellington) depicts the lower end of Church Hill, looking east towards the former parish church on the left. The sender of the card wrote on the back, 'This is the road leading to the church; you will notice the houses are nearly all one storey, the sleeping arrangements are a niche in the wall round which they draw a curtain. Very snug in winters but our boys say they are very hot in summer. The children wear no boots and stocking but it's funny these here have them on.'

Old maps show this part of Church Hill as Church Street, the part beyond to the left being known as High Church Street. The old road from Dalmellington to New Cumnock went this way, climbing up part of Mains Hill before traversing the hillside and dropping to a bridge over the Cummock Burn, near Pennyvenie. This road passed Camlarg House, much to the annoyance of the owners, so they arranged for a new roadway to be built along the north side of the Cummock Burn for two miles, before crossing the Cummock bridge and passing by way of Gillies Knowe and entering the village at High Main Street. This may have happened soon after 1774, when the road was formally established by the Ayr turnpike act.

At the start of the First World War, roughly when this picture was taken, the buildings to the right were occupied by James Hill; a bakery operated by Dalmellington Industrial Co-operative Society; Quintin Pettigrew, collier; John Riddock, sexton; James Orr, collier; and the last house, known as the Keeper's House, by Mrs Jane MacCubbin, widow. As with a number of old properties around Dalmellington, some of the cottages had byres to the rear (such as that occupied by John Riddock), where they kept cattle. The cows could be grazed on the Town's Common, near Bellsbank farm, or else in small fields rented from the local landowners. The building to the left of centre was owned by George Gibson, a builder who lived at Knowehead, and it was occupied by a widow, Mrs Mary Watt.

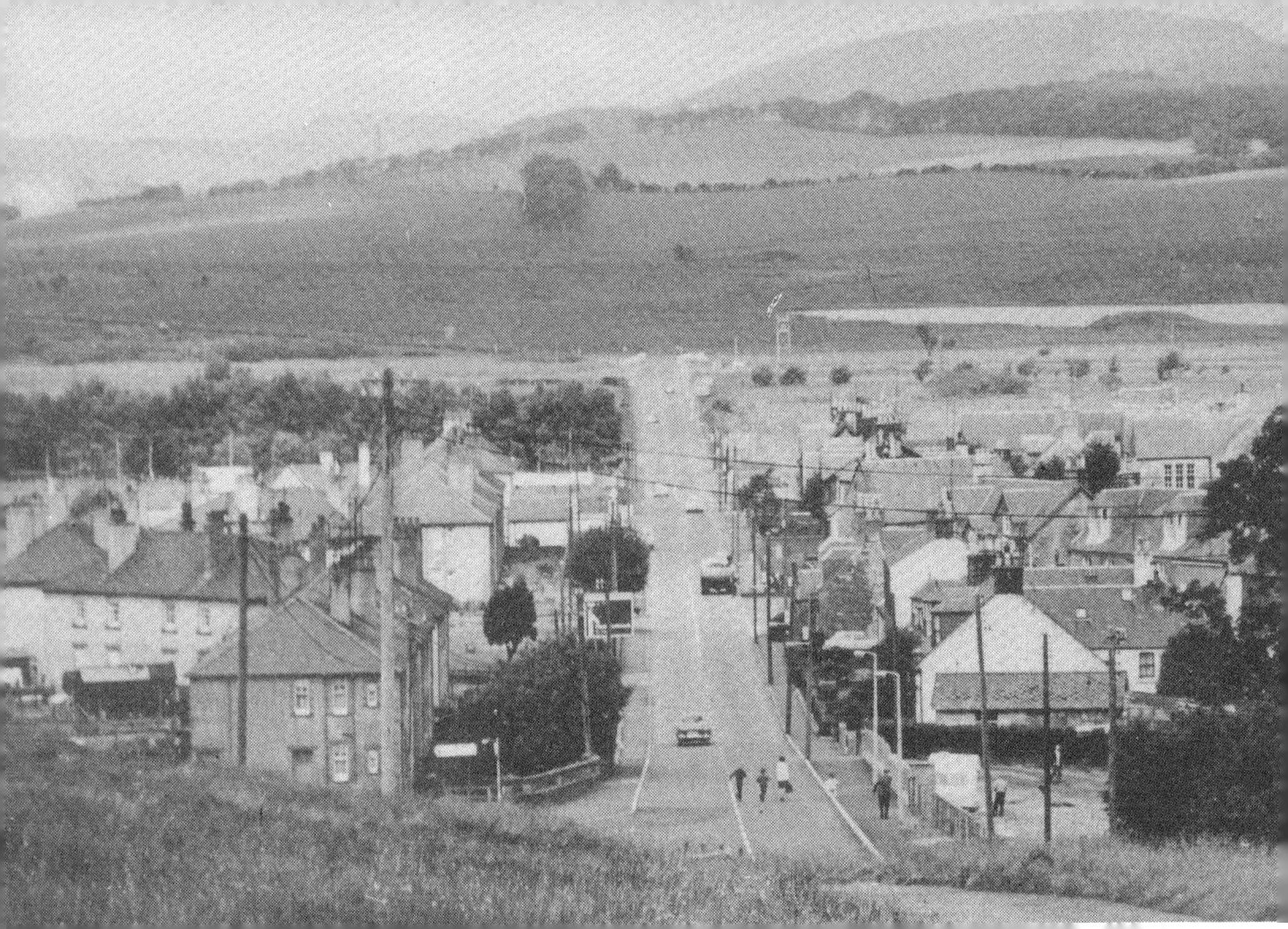

Bellsbank Road

This postcard view of Dalmellington was taken from near the war memorial, looking north-west along Bellsbank Road and Ayr Road towards the lower Doon valley, with the Green Hill of Dunaksin rising beyond. This hill is topped with an ancient burial cairn, indicating its importance in prehistoric times. The cairn measured 23 paces in diameter and rose four feet in height when John Smith, author of *Prehistoric Man in Ayrshire*, visited in the late nineteenth century.

Bellsbank Road was originally only built up on its northern side, the cottages there often being built in the back riggs or gardens of the buildings in Main Street. The south side was an open field until it was selected for the erection of council houses, seen to the left of the picture. These houses were erected to rehouse people from older cottages which had been condemned as being unsuitable for human habitation.

The western continuation of Bellsbank Road is known as Ayr Road. In it the new school was built in 1874, the police station in 1876-77 (designed by John Murdoch), and a drill hall for the Ayrshire Territorial Force Association. Here at various times was Ivy Dean Dairy, St Inan (Products) Ltd, manufacturers of hornware, an Indian takeaway and Ayr Road Garage. A number of large villas were also erected here, such as Glenauchie, for the Williamson family of Beoch farm, and Ivydean, for John Murray, draper.

Just visible, where the road strikes to the left, is a tower associated with the aerial ropeway which transported coal from Bogton Pit to the Burnton Washery Plant. This was a rather distinguishing feature of the Dalmellington vicinity and operated from around 1935 to the mid-1950s. Coal was transported in containers suspended from ropes, the line passing over the Burnton area, and on windy days some coal was spilled from the containers. Children used to gather this free coal and take it home to their parents. When the aerial ropeway was no longer required it was dismantled and taken to Butlin's holiday camp at Ayr, where it was rebuilt in 1959 as a chair lift, transporting holidaymakers over the campsite.

Acknowledgments

I would like to thank a variety of people who have kindly supplied pictures and snippets of information that have been used in this book. They include Elaine Mackie at the Doon Valley Museum, which was closed by East Ayrshire Council in January 2017, and Ian Riggans. The other pictures are from the author's own collection. I would also like to thank the many people who have supplied information to me over the years - often these notes are filed away, to be used at some time in the future.